500 FACTS

WORLD WAR II HISTORY
FOR KIDS

Major Events, Pivotal Victories, and Acts of Heroism—from Europe to the Pacific

KELLY MILNER HALLS

Illustrated by Katy Dockrill

ROCKRIDGE
PRESS

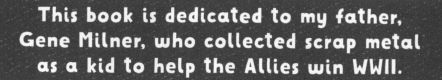

This book is dedicated to my father, Gene Milner, who collected scrap metal as a kid to help the Allies win WWII.

For general information on our other products and services or to obtain technical support, please contact our Customer Care Department within the United States at (866) 744-2665, or outside the United States at (510) 253-0500.

Rockridge Press publishes its books in a variety of electronic and print formats. Some content that appears in print may not be available in electronic books, and vice versa.

TRADEMARKS: Rockridge Press and the Rockridge Press logo are trademarks or registered trademarks of Callisto Media Inc. and/or its affiliates, in the United States and other countries, and may not be used without written permission. All other trademarks are the property of their respective owners. Rockridge Press is not associated with any product or vendor mentioned in this book.

Series Designer: Tricia Jang
Interior and Cover Designer: Linda Snorina
Art Producer: Meg Baggott
Editor: Laura Bryn Sisson
Production Manager: Martin Worthington
Production Editor: Melissa Edeburn

Illustrations © 2021 Katy Dockrill
Author photo courtesy of Roxyanne Young

Paperback ISBN: 978-1-64876-376-2
eBook ISBN: 978-1-64876-377-9
R0

CONTENTS

INTRODUCTION

World War II lasted six years and one day. From September 1, 1939, to September 2, 1945, nearly 70 million men and women fought to determine how everyone around the globe would live. Great Britain, France, China, and, later, the United States and the Soviet Union fought together as the chief Allied powers to defeat the Axis powers. The three main Axis powers of Germany, Italy, and Japan fought to expand their territory and destroy Soviet communism.

Most history books recount the story of this epic struggle with a list of names and dates. But this book provides 500 facts about fascinating people and shocking events that bring those names and dates to life.

Some facts will amaze you. Did you know more than 40 billion bullets were fired during the war? Some facts will make you sad. It's hard not to feel sorrowful knowing nearly 40 million people died over six battle-torn years. But some facts might even make you smile. After all, a brown bear named Wojtek served in the Polish army and got double servings of food!

Get ready to dive into 500 facts about World War II. You might never see them on a test at school, but they will make learning about the war a lot more interesting.

CHAPTER 1

BEFORE THE WAR
(1914-1929)

The world had grown tired of war and killing before World War II even started. Hundreds of billions of dollars were spent fighting World War I just a few decades earlier. Millions of people had been killed. Millions more were wounded and forever changed. People were ready to move past the sorrows of war. They wanted peace and normal life to return. But nothing felt normal. Food was harder to find because most men had been fighting instead of growing and harvesting crops to eat. Jobs disappeared, and so did paychecks. People wanted help and answers, but they were not easy to find.

- When American soldiers came home from World War I, they received only $60 to buy new clothes.

- In World War I, many soldiers were wounded in the face when they peeked their heads above trenches to fire guns.

- Breakthroughs in plastic surgery resulted from World War I. Surgeons created new ways to repair soldiers' wounded faces.

World War I

PEOPLE TO KNOW **ARCHDUKE FRANZ FERDINAND** and his wife, Sophie, were the rulers of Austria-Hungary before World War I. When they were murdered by political assassins in 1914, World War I began.

Germany, Austria-Hungary, Bulgaria, and the Ottoman Empire joined together to fight. They were known as the Central powers.

The Allied powers fought against the Central powers in World War I. The Allies included the United States, Great Britain, France, Russia, Italy, Romania, and Japan.

ALLIED FORCES   CENTRAL POWERS

TERM TO KNOW Before World War I, many battles were fought on horseback, but soldiers in WWI engaged in **TRENCH WARFARE**. They fought from deep ditches dug in the earth and used rifles and bombs.

➡ Allied trenches were muddy and full of rats. The harsh conditions led to widespread sickness. Central powers trenches were safer. Some even had electricity.

STAT FACT In the 1916 Battle of Somme, more than **20,000** British soldiers were killed in a single day of trench warfare.

Negotiating Peace

➡ Germany surrendered in November 1918. The other Central powers agreed to stop fighting while a peace agreement was written.

TERM TO KNOW The peace agreement was called the **TREATY OF VERSAILLES**. It was signed in Paris, France, in June 1919 with the leaders of the United States, Great Britain, France, and Italy in key positions to create the new rules and national borders.

Children playing with worthless German money

STAT FACT Germany was ordered to pay Allied nations **132 BILLION GOLD MARKS** for the damage it had caused. That's almost **270 BILLION DOLLARS** today. Germany did not have the money. Suddenly, their dollars were worth only pennies.

♦ US President Woodrow Wilson proposed the League of Nations, a group of world leaders dedicated to ending international disputes before they became wars. A total of 58 member states or countries joined.

Palais Wilson in Geneva, first League of Nations headquarters

♦ The League of Nations declared that aggressive war was a crime against all of humanity. They set up a court in the Geneva, Switzerland, headquarters to examine those crimes.

♦ The Big Three leaders of the League of Nations were supposed to be the United States, Great Britain, and France. But the US Congress voted not to join President Wilson's international creation.

The Flu Pandemic

STAT FACT An influenza pandemic swept the world in 1918. At least **50 MILLION** people died.

➡ The flu was called the Spanish Flu, but it did not come from Spain. Spain was the first nation to report the deadly flu because they were not fighting in World War I. Other nations kept their flu cases a secret at first.

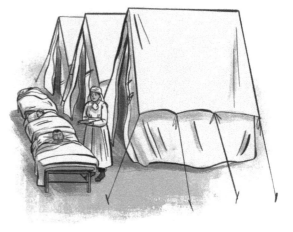

Temporary hospitals

US President Woodrow Wilson got the flu during the peace talks after World War I.

➡ When President Wilson had the flu, his doctor lied to the public. He said it was a bad cold. But Wilson was confined to bed for days with a fever of 103 degrees Fahrenheit.

⭐ Wearing masks was the only way to slow the spread of the virus. Those who refused to wear them were called "mask slackers" and often fined $5.

➡ The flu vaccine wasn't developed until 1933, after microscopes became powerful enough for scientists to see and study the influenza virus.

Worldwide Depression

STAT FACT World War I was a very expensive war to fight. It cost **$208 BILLION**, and most of the expense fell to European nations.

◆ After World War I ended, American leaders wanted their war allies to repay their debts. The only way Great Britain and France could find the money to pay the United States was to collect it from Germany.

Soup line

◆ Germany had been ordered to pay hefty fines for their part in the war, but their economy was weak, too. They couldn't pay Great Britain and France, so America couldn't collect what it was owed.

TERM TO KNOW By 1929, America's economy had crashed. This time was known as the **GREAT DEPRESSION**. Money and jobs were scarce all over the world.

★ Food was hard to come by, so people ate differently. In the United States, the casserole was born. Take some chopped beef, add boiled peas, and top it off with a white sauce made of flour, milk, salt, and butter. Chipped beef was filling and cheap.

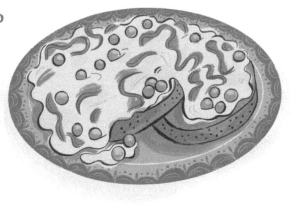

Chipped beef on toast

★ In Europe, pasta and tomato sauce helped keep people fed when money and food were scarce. The dish was simple, tasty, and nutritious.

The Rise of Hitler

PERSON TO KNOW Germany, known as Prussia, was ruled by **KAISER WILHELM II** until World War I ended. When Germany lost the war, he was forced to **ABDICATE**, or leave, his royal throne.

→ Germany tried to form a democracy called the Weimar Republic. But there was no clear majority after the people voted. Some people wanted a democracy, and others wanted military rule or different forms of government.

Coat of arms of the Weimar Republic

→ Without one ideology in power, the government was unstable. That instability gave Adolf Hitler and his Nazi Party a chance to rise to power.

TERM TO KNOW Adolf Hitler and his Nazi Party started attracting greater public interest around 1921. But it was in November 1923 that they made their first push for real power. They tried to take over the German state of Bavaria in an event called the **BEER HALL PUTSCH**.

→ Hitler was convicted of treason after the Beer Hall Putsch. He was sentenced to five years in prison, but he served less than one year.

Hitler wrote his autobiography while he was in jail. It was called *Mein Kampf*, which means "my struggle."

Adolf Hitler

Fascism

TERM TO KNOW **FASCISM** is the belief that one leader should have complete control over what happens in their country, without advice from its citizens. It is rooted in strong national pride.

◆ Fascism became popular after World War I because the people in Germany thought their leaders were weak when they negotiated the Treaty of Versailles. The idea of one strong leader seemed more promising.

★ The word "fascism" comes from *fascio*, the Italian word for bundle. Ancient Roman leaders held a bundle of wood with an ax blade attached to it, which was called a fasces.

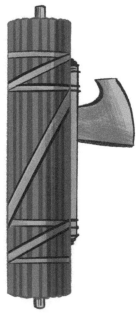

Fasces

TERM TO KNOW **AUTHORITARIAN** is a word for a tyrant who rules by their own will, instead of listening to the will of the people within their country or region.

PERSON TO KNOW **BENITO MUSSOLINI** introduced his fascist political party, Fasci Italiani di Combattimento, to Italy in March 1919. It was a new name for a violent kind of authoritarianism. Thousands of people were killed in Mussolini's bid to gain control of the country.

→ Mussolini believed democracy did not work. He thought people should be dedicated to whatever he believed was good for Italy, rather than having beliefs of their own.

Flag of Mussolini's Italy

Dictators

TERM TO KNOW A **DICTATOR** is an authoritarian, or a leader who believes their actions determine the law without any debate or vote to change that law. A dictator has total control.

➧ Most dictators make sweeping promises that appeal to people. They might say everyone will have a job and enough food to eat. But they generally don't keep these promises.

After World War I, three dictators took over European countries: Mussolini ruled Italy, Hitler ruled Germany, and General Francisco Franco ruled Spain.

Symbol of Francoism in Spain

◆ Mussolini had an army of violent police called the Blackshirts. They swept through Italy killing or jailing anyone who opposed his dictatorship.

TERM TO KNOW **SOCIALISM** means the good of every individual comes before the good of one leader. Both Hitler and Mussolini said they were socialists when they first rose to power, but they were both lying.

PERSON TO KNOW Japanese **EMPEROR HIROHITO** was raised to believe he was the leader chosen by God. He was not a true dictator, but the leaders of his military adopted fascism after World War I. He probably backed them up just to stay alive.

Emperor Hirohito

CHAPTER 2

A GOAL TO RULE THE WORLD

(1925–1939)

With the world in a postwar state of confusion, power-hungry leaders saw opportunity. If they struck quickly, global power might be within reach—especially if they formed alliances. People were so busy trying to survive and put food on the table that they hardly noticed their freedom was disappearing. Bad times can make bad things seem normal. Bad times can also make it easy for selfish people to gain powerful positions through dishonesty. And once they are in power, they can be hard to take down.

- In March 1932, Adolf Hitler ran for president representing the National Socialist German Workers Party, also called the Nazis.

- Hitler did not win the 1932 election. President Paul von Hindenburg won about half the German vote.

- Hindenburg got the most votes, but it was not enough of a majority to form a government.

Hitler and Hindenburg

➤ Hindenburg was a wealthy war hero and authoritarian who won the German presidency in February 1925. But his government was unstable and he needed political allies to fix it.

STAT FACT Hindenburg didn't approve of the Nazi Party or their tactics, but Hitler won **37.4 PERCENT** of the German vote in 1932.

The German president saw that Hitler was clearly gaining popularity. Although Hindenburg did not like Hitler, he decided to try to form an alliance with him.

Crowds gathered to hear Hitler speak

The Führer

◆ President Hindenburg proposed an alliance with Hitler after the German election in 1932. In exchange for joining forces, Hitler demanded the title of German chancellor. He was offered the vice-chancellor position instead. Hitler refused. Advisers told Hindenburg to give in to Hitler's demand.

Hitler was appointed chancellor in January 1933.

Hitler shaking hands with Hindenburg

◆ Hindenburg thought he could control Hitler behind the scenes. He thought there were enough non-Nazis in the government to stop Hitler's brutal ambitions. He was wrong.

◆ The Nazi Party won two seats in the German parliament, so Hitler appointed his allies to the seats. He named the head of the police and the head of the interior. These powerful positions helped the Nazis gain total control of the country.

After Hitler was appointed chancellor, the Enabling Act was passed in March 1933. It gave Hitler the same powers as Hindenburg.

When Hindenburg died in August 1934, Hitler gave himself the combined power of president and chancellor. He became the Führer.

Führer is the German word for "leader."

The motto of the Nazis became "ein Volk, ein Reich, ein Führer," which meant "one people, one nation, one leader." The phrase was printed on posters. Hitler was an all-powerful dictator.

The Axis Forms

On May 22, 1939, Hitler and Mussolini agreed their countries would not go to war against each other by signing the Pact of Steel. It was the first step toward forming the Axis powers of World War II.

Signing of German-Soviet Nonaggression Pact

PERSON TO KNOW **JOSEPH STALIN** was the communist leader of the Soviet Union. He knew Hitler hated communists, but he still signed the German-Soviet Nonaggression Pact on August 23, 1939.

TERM TO KNOW **COMMUNISM** is the idea that property, like land and houses, should be owned by everyone, and each person should be paid what they need for the work they do.

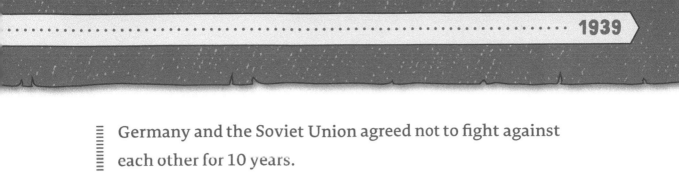

Germany and the Soviet Union agreed not to fight against each other for 10 years.

On September 27, 1940, Japan joined the Axis powers by signing the Tripartite Pact. With the treaty, Japan promised not to fight Italy or Germany. They signed a pact with the Soviet Union in April 1941.

Signing of the Soviet-Japanese Neutrality Pact

★ Spain was considered neutral, meaning it did not officially side with any country. But Spanish dictator Francisco Franco was a secret ally to Adolf Hitler and the Nazis.

Secret Weapons

⭐ The Horten Ho 229 was a prototype for a stealth bomber plane that would carry 2,000 pounds of bombs. It never saw combat.

Horten Ho

STAT FACT The Fritz X was a radio-controlled bomb that could be sent to any location to cut through **28 INCHES** of metal armor. It was dropped from **20,000 FEET** in the sky—beyond the reach of anti-aircraft guns.

⭐ The Goliath was a small remote-control vehicle designed to deliver explosives. American forces nicknamed it "Doodlebug."

Germany created the Messerschmitt Me 163 Komet fighter jet, complete with two massive cannons. It could fly 700 miles per hour.

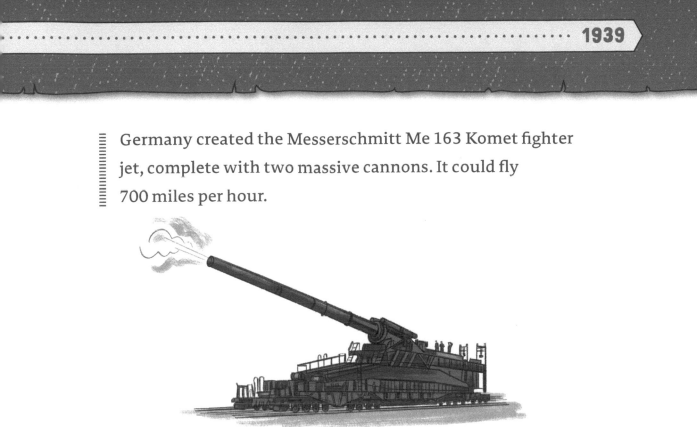

Gustav gun

STAT FACT Hitler's Gustav railway gun was **40 FEET** tall and weighed **1,350 TONS**. It was designed to fire a **10,000-POUND** rocket that would destroy concrete barriers. But its size made it an easy target for Allied bomber planes.

➡ The Henschel Hs 117 Schmetterling was a radio-controlled ground-to-air missile guided by a joystick. *Schmetterling* is the German word for "butterfly."

Prewar Attacks

◆ Japan began to expand into China when it invaded Manchuria in 1931. Japan's island geography meant Japan had limited natural resources. It wanted territory in China in order to take their resources.

◆ In 1936, the Nazis invaded the Rhineland, a neutral zone along the Rhine River in Central Europe. Hitler violated the Treaty of Versailles when he claimed it for Germany.

◆ Japan continued its occupation of China on July 7, 1937, when it invaded Beijing in northern China. Japan's secretary of state urged Japan's military to restrain the violence, but they ignored him.

Hitler quietly took over Austria on March 12, 1938. The combined territory of Germany and Austria was called the Anschluss.

STAT FACT The German air force was called the Luftwaffe. When they attacked Wielun, Poland, on September 1, 1939, it was a war crime. The Luftwaffe dropped **380 BOMBS** on **16,000** innocent people.

Luftwaffe

TERM TO KNOW The sudden aerial bombings of Germany's Luftwaffe became known as **BLITZKRIEG** attacks. *Blitzkrieg* means "lightning war." The attacks were later used in Belgium, North Africa, the Netherlands, France, and Great Britain.

Escalation to War

➡ When Hitler claimed Austria in 1938, Great Britain's Prime Minister Neville Chamberlain offered Hitler a compromise known as the Munich Agreement. It gave Hitler permission to invade a part of Czechoslovakia, but only if he promised to stop there.

Chamberlain shaking hands with Hitler

PERSON TO KNOW British military leader **WINSTON CHURCHILL**, who would soon become prime minister, opposed the compromise. He described it as a "disaster" and said it was dishonorable to give in to Hitler.

Hitler broke the Munich Agreement in March 1939 by conquering all of Czechoslovakia.

- On September 1, 1939, Hitler invaded Poland from the west, claiming Poland had attacked Germany first. He had lied. On September 17, 1939, Stalin's armies invaded Poland from the east.

Soviet invasion of Poland

- Great Britain and France had a military treaty with Poland. The agreement to defend Poland if it ever came under attack forced both nations to declare war on Germany on September 3, 1939.

TERM TO KNOW The United States believed in **ISOLATIONISM**, which meant America wanted to take care of its own concerns without becoming involved in other countries' disagreements. Most Americans believed the fight in Europe had nothing to do with them.

CHAPTER 3
HITLER'S NAZI GERMANY
(1933-1945)

After President Hindenburg appointed Hitler as chancellor of Germany, change was swift. In 1933, the Reichstag building that housed the German government went up in flames when someone set a fire. Hitler blamed his political enemy: the Communist Party. He convinced the German public that the Communists had committed the arson attack to overthrow the government. In response, Hindenburg quickly passed the Reichstag Fire Decree. This new law gave Hitler more power. "There will be no mercy now," said the Nazi police commander soon after the decree was set. "Anyone who stands in our way will be cut down."

- The Reichstag Fire Decree suspended the individual rights of German people.

- People could be arrested and jailed without evidence or proof.

- The national government, controlled by Nazi police, could ignore regional laws and do whatever Hitler wanted them to do.

Hitler's Psychic

- In 1909, when Hitler was 20, he became fascinated by the supernatural after meeting an author named Jörg Lanz von Liebenfels. Liebenfels believed a supernatural race of "God Men" would one day rule the world.

- In 1932, a psychic called Erik Jan Hanussen told Hitler he would be given great power in 30 days if Hanussen found a mandrake root from Hitler's birthplace.

Erik Jan Hanussen leading a seance

Hanussen retrieved a mandrake root from Hitler's birthplace on New Year's Day, 1933. Thirty days later, Hitler was named chancellor of Germany.

Hitler's Mission

German politics were in chaos in the 1930s. As many as 30 different parties were on the election ballots.

→ The Communist Party was on the liberal side of German politics. The National Socialists, also known as the Nazi Party, were on the ultra-conservative side. The Catholic Center, Social Democrats, Democrats, and People's Party were a few parties in the middle.

→ The vote was divided in the 1932 German election. There was no clear majority, so a coalition government was formed with Hitler and Hindenburg. Power was awarded to both sides.

Ballot in 1932 German election

→ Hitler blamed the Communist Party for the Reichstag fire, so Germans turned on the party. By March 1933, 10,000 German communists had been arrested.

Nazi flags soon appeared in German government windows and on German streets. Hitler designed the flags himself.

→ In January 1933, Hindenburg appointed Hitler as chancellor of Germany. A second election in March helped Hitler gather enough power to overthrow Hindenburg's government and move closer to total control.

Education in the Third Reich

TERM TO KNOW The Nazis used misinformation or lies, called **PROPAGANDA**, to control the German people. Joseph Goebbels was the Nazi Minister of Public Enlightenment and Propaganda.

▶ On May 10, 1933, Goebbels convinced German college students to burn more than 25,000 books. Authors whose books were burned included Albert Einstein, Sigmund Freud, Ernest Hemingway, Helen Keller, Jack London, Karl Marx, Heinrich Heine, and others. Protesters called the burning an "action against the un-German spirit."

★ American newspapers protested Nazi book burning with editorial cartoons, including some drawn by Dr. Seuss.

- The Nazis taught young Germans they would please Hitler by joining a boys' club called the Hitler Youth and a girls' club called the League of German Maidens.

- In public school, children learned about the rise of the Nazi Party in history classes. Geography classes taught that countries near Germany were weak. Biology classes taught a lie claiming the white "Aryan" race was better than all other races.

- Fitness was important to the Nazis. Schoolchildren had to do five hours of physical education every week, often in two-hour sessions. Boxing was mandatory for boys.

Third Reich Economy

STAT FACT When Hitler took power in 1933, **6 MILLION** Germans, or **33 PERCENT** of the nation's adult population, were out of work.

→ Hitler lied by saying the unemployment rate in Germany was down. He used misleading numbers that did not include unemployed women and unemployed Jews.

→ Men who were searching for full-time jobs to support a family were forced to take lesser jobs to make them seem fully employed. If they refused, they were sent to concentration camps.

TERM TO KNOW **CONCENTRATION CAMPS** were horrific Nazi prisons. It wasn't just unemployed men who were imprisoned there. Millions of men, women, and children died in these camps. The victims were mostly Jewish but also included communists, LGBTQ+ people, political prisoners, and many others.

→ The Treaty of Versailles banned Germany from producing weapons after World War I ended. But Hitler ignored the treaty. Instead, he ordered the production of tanks, aircraft, and ships.

Making war machines required natural resources, including iron and oil. More German jobs were created to source, mine, and manufacture with these resources.

→ Hitler created the National Labor Service, which required all unemployed men ages 18 to 25 to labor on public works projects.

The Master Race

→ Some German women were part of the workforce, but Hitler encouraged all white German women to marry, stay home, and give birth to lots of white children. He wanted to build a "master race" to populate the world.

TERM TO KNOW The **ARYAN NATION** was the "master race" of white people Hitler wanted to create. It was inspired by a supernatural fiction writer he met as a young man.

★ White German women who had multiple children received a medal called the Cross of Honour of the German Mother. Mothers of five won the bronze medal. Mothers of six or seven won the silver medal. Women with eight or more children won the gold.

Cross of Honor
of the German Mother

TERM TO KNOW **ANTISEMITISM** is the disrespect or ill treatment of Jewish people, an ethnoreligious group that at the time had significant populations in Europe. As early as 1919, Hitler wrote about his antisemitic vision for a world without Jewish people. He said, "The ultimate goal must definitely be the removal of the Jews altogether."

Jewish people under threat by Nazi soldier

◆ Hitler and many other Germans believed Jewish people helped the Allies win World War I by investing money in Allied military. It was not true, but spreading the lie made it easier for Hitler to convince angry people to blame the Jews.

STAT FACT Hitler passed more than **400** rules to take away Jewish rights, properties, and freedoms.

Nazi Leaders

PERSON TO KNOW **HEINRICH HIMMLER** was chief of the German police, known as the SS, and the minister of the interior. He was the second most powerful Nazi, and he was in charge of killing Europe's Jewish population.

PERSON TO KNOW **HERMANN GÖRING** helped Hitler overthrow the German Republic in favor of Nazi rule. He commanded the Luftwaffe and created a secret Nazi police division called the Gestapo.

Heinrich Himmler

PERSON TO KNOW **JOSEPH GOEBBELS** had polio as a child, which left him with a disabled leg. He could not fight in battle for Hitler, but he could spread Nazi propaganda. Goebbels was in charge of Nazi radio, newspapers, and fine arts.

PERSON TO KNOW **MARTIN BORMANN** ran the head office of the Nazi Party and was Hitler's private secretary. Bormann's son was Hitler's godson. Not a scrap of information got to Hitler unless Bormann approved it first.

PERSON TO KNOW **WILHELM KEITEL** was Hitler's chief of staff and the head of the German army, known as the Wehrmacht. His fellow officers disliked him because he allowed Hitler to shape military policies, even when these policies were faulty.

Martin Bormann

PERSON TO KNOW Field Marshal **ERICH VON MANSTEIN** was probably Hitler's most powerful general. Manstein helped Hitler betray his Soviet Union allies and attempt a takeover of their territories.

The Gestapo

TERM TO KNOW The Nazis had a secret police force called the **GESTAPO**. Officers for the Gestapo searched for enemies of Hitler and violently destroyed them.

➤ At first, the Gestapo was formed to protect Nazi officers from their political enemies. They soon evolved into a murderous force with few limits. Laws did not apply to the Gestapo.

STAT FACT By March 1937, the Gestapo employed **6,500** people in **54** regional offices across Nazi-held territories. These offices rounded up Jewish people and sent them to Nazi concentration camps to work, suffer, and die.

Gestapo flag

The Sicherheitsdienst, also known as the SD, was a bloodthirsty security service. It partnered with the Gestapo.

Heinrich Himmler and Hermann Göring were in a power struggle to see who would win control of all Nazi enforcement agents (people who enforced Hitler's laws) in Germany and German-occupied lands. Himmler won the fight in 1934.

Officially, the Gestapo was created to protect the Nazi Party from German traitors. But the Gestapo grew to be the brutal law-enforcement tool in German-occupied territories.

Gestapo officer

Nazi Symbols

♦ SS police wore a decorative hat pin called the Totenkopf. It looked like a human skull made of silver metal. *Totenkopf* means "death's head." It was first used in the 1700s by Prussian leader Frederick the Great.

♦ SS officers also wore the silver Reichsadler pin. It showed a heraldic eagle. The same eagle grasping a Nazi swastika became the German national emblem in 1935.

Totenkopf

SS officers, Nazi soldiers, and Nazi civilians wore red cotton armbands marked with black symbols called swastikas to show their loyalty to Hitler.

◆ Nazi soldiers could earn different badges for their uniforms. These badges gave the illusion of individuality.

★ Hitler created a 70-page guide to emphasize the importance of graphic design. Images and propaganda played a big part in the Nazi uprising.

▤ Hitler's government passed the Nazi Law for Protection of National Symbols. It controlled where the swastika could be used and where it was forbidden.

CHAPTER 4

THE HOLOCAUST
(1933-1945)

It's hard to determine exactly how Adolf Hitler grew to hate Jewish people. For most of his life he didn't outwardly show disrespect for those in this ethnoreligious group. But at some point, he came to believe that Jewish money caused Germany to lose World War I. His anger intensified as Germans struggled to survive after the war. Hitler was not the only angry citizen. Others were looking for someone to blame for their poverty and personal losses. Hitler's fiery speeches encouraged them to blame the Jews. These lies helped Hitler gain political power. And as he grew stronger, Hitler's desire to drive Jews out of Germany transformed into a desire to see them dead.

- Before he entered politics, Hitler wrote and gave speeches for the German army.

- Hitler said that a propaganda speech should "confine itself to a few points and repeat them over and over."

- The Nazi policy of exterminating Jewish people was called the "Final Solution."

Hitler Targets Jews

◆ The Nazis organized a boycott of Jewish businesses in Germany on April 1, 1933. Nazi officers stood in front of these establishments saying, "Don't buy from Jews." It lasted only one day, but it was the start of an evil plan.

◆ Hitler banned Jews and other people proclaimed "Nazi enemies" from working for the government on April 7, 1933.

By September 30, 1933, Jews were banned from practicing law in Germany.

Nazi boycott of Jewish businesses

STAT FACT Only **5 PERCENT** of students in German public schools could be Jewish. The rest of the Jewish students were forced to attend private Jewish schools.

Night of Broken Glass

Kristallnacht

◆ On November 9, 1938, Nazi soldiers, police, and members of the Hitler Youth attacked Jewish businesses across Germany. It became known as Kristallnacht, or the Night of Broken Glass.

STAT FACT More than **7,000** Jewish-owned businesses were robbed, vandalized, and closed. Their shattered glass windows were the basis for the name of the terrorist event.

TERM TO KNOW A **SYNAGOGUE** is a Jewish place of worship. Synagogues were burned to the ground during Kristallnacht. Nazi firefighters watched as the holy places were turned to ash. They only fought to save "Aryan" properties.

STAT FACT More than **100** Jewish Germans were killed during the violent riots. Another **30,000** Jewish men were jailed and deported to concentration camps. Dozens took their own lives when faced with the horrors of Nazi abuse.

➡ Jewish cemeteries were vandalized or destroyed by Nazi supporters.

TERM TO KNOW After the Night of Broken Glass, some Jews abandoned their homes and tried to move to safer locations. But most of Europe soon turned against their Jewish citizens.

A burning synagogue on Kristallnacht

Ghettos

TERM TO KNOW The word **GHETTO** came from Italy, where in 1516 the ruling class of Venice forced Jewish people to live in isolation away from Christian citizens.

Life in the ghettos

STAT FACT The Nazis isolated Jews in occupied Europe, setting up at least **1,143** ghettos.

➤ Hitler set up three kinds of ghettos. Closed ghettos were walled off and people could not leave. Open ghettos had no walls, but Jews could leave only if granted permission. Destruction ghettos jailed Jews until they were put to death.

STAT FACT The largest ghetto was in Warsaw, Poland. More than **400,000** Jews were forced to live in an area that was only **1.3 SQUARE MILES.**

TERM TO KNOW Nazis appointed imprisoned Jewish men to the **JUDENRAETE**. It was like a Jewish city council group within the ghetto. They were told to enforce Nazi rules inside the walls. If they didn't obey, they were killed and replaced.

→ When the Nazis adopted the "Final Solution," they destroyed the ghettos and murdered the Jews inside. Those not killed in the ghettos were forced to work, and often die, in concentration camps.

Closed ghettos

Life in the Ghetto

Jewish citizens were forced to wear a yellow badge shaped like a Star of David on their clothes. Nazis used the badge to separate Jews from other citizens.

◆ Nazis confined their Jewish captives in as little space as possible. This overcrowding caused a flood of human waste to fill the ghetto streets. That waste not only caused the ghetto to smell and grow filthier, but it also attracted insects and rats that quickly spread disease.

◆ Jews in ghettos had very little food or medicine, so disease hit them much harder than it might have affected well-fed people with proper medical care.

**Jewish children forced to wear the
Star of David on their clothes**

→ Older people were the most vulnerable to contagious diseases that spread through the ghettos. The children they left behind were orphans. No one remained to care for them.

TERM TO KNOW One of the deadliest diseases in the ghetto was **TYPHUS**, which was spread by bites from fleas and rats. Once a person was infected, they suffered from fever and body aches. Nausea, vomiting, and loss of appetite came next. Then came a cough, a red rash, and finally death.

If Germans living nearby were infected with typhus, Jews in the ghettos had to take disinfection baths to protect their Nazi neighbors.

German Resistance

TERM TO KNOW **GLEICHSCHALTUNG** was Hitler's plan to force ordinary German people to act like Nazis. Many Germans supported it, but some were opposed.

> Many German citizens were members of the Catholic Church. So were many Nazi officers.

PERSON TO KNOW The Catholic Church and the Nazis agreed to share power over Catholic Germans and other European Catholics as they spread across the continent. But some Catholic leaders, like **MONSIGNOR HUGH O'FLAHERTY**, joined the resistance against the Nazis and worked to save their Jewish neighbors.

Monsignor Hugh O'Flaherty

➡ Some young Germans forced to join Hitler's youth groups fought the Nazis in secret. A group called the White Rose spread anti-Nazi fliers to encourage resistance.

PERSON TO KNOW A 36-year-old Nazi officer named **COLONEL CLAUS SCHENK GRAF VON STAUFFENBERG** tried to assassinate Hitler by placing a bomb inside a briefcase and leaving it in Hitler's secret headquarters. The bomb exploded on July 20, 1944, but Hitler survived. Stauffenberg was executed for the attempt.

➡ A group of teenagers called the Churchill Club resisted the Nazis in Denmark. They blew up Nazi trucks while riding bicycles and made it home in time for dinner.

Notable People

Anne Frank

PERSON TO KNOW **ANNE FRANK** was 13 when she and her Jewish family went into hiding in Amsterdam in 1942. Two years later, they were discovered by the Nazis. Anne and most of her family died at the Bergen-Belsen concentration camp when Anne was 15.

PERSON TO KNOW **MARCEL MARCEAU** was a famous mime artist. But as a young man in France, he saved Jewish children from the Nazis after the soldiers murdered his father.

PERSON TO KNOW **HANS AND SOPHIE SCHOLL** formed the White Rose resistance group in Germany to fight Hitler from within the country. They were executed for placing anti-Nazi fliers in public places.

Josephine Baker

PERSON TO KNOW

JOSEPHINE BAKER was a world-famous African-American entertainer who lived in France. She worked for the French Resistance by spying on Nazi officers who came to watch her perform in Paris.

PERSON TO KNOW **HELMUTH HÜBENER** was a German Boy Scout and member of the Mormon church who opposed the Nazis. He was only 17 when the Nazis beheaded him for writing anti-Nazi pamphlets.

PERSON TO KNOW **ELIE WIESEL** and his family lived in Jewish ghettos but were transferred to a Nazi death camp called Auschwitz when Elie was only 15. His parents and young sister did not survive, but he later became an acclaimed writer and won the Nobel Prize.

Survival Stories

TERM TO KNOW **KINDERTRANSPORT** was the word used to describe the rescue of thousands of Jewish children threatened by the Nazis.

→ Between November 1938 and September 1939, kids ages 5 to 17 left their families in Germany, Austria, Poland, and Czechoslovakia to live with people in England.

STAT FACT More than **10,000** children were saved, but many never saw their parents again.

PERSON TO KNOW **BRUNO TOUSCHEK** was a university student when he was arrested by the Gestapo in 1945. As he marched to a concentration camp, he was shot and left for dead. He survived and went on to become a famous physicist.

PERSON TO KNOW **ROBERT CLARY** was 12 when he started singing professionally for French radio in 1938. Four years later, he barely clung to life in a concentration camp. He survived to become an actor and star in an American television comedy called *Hogan's Heroes*, about life in a Nazi prisoner-of-war camp.

Robert Clary (left) in *Hogan's Heroes*

STAT FACT Chaim Ferster, who was from Poland, survived **EIGHT** concentration camps.

Concentration Camps

The first concentration camp was called Dachau. It opened in March 1933 and ran until April 1945.

STAT FACT **In addition to concentration camps, the Nazis created forced-labor camps, temporary prisons called transit camps, and prisoner-of-war camps. They also had killing centers. From 1943 to 1944, 6,000 Jews died in gas chambers at killing centers every day. More than 2,772,000 Jews died in camps during World War II.**

Auschwitz was a place of death, but midwife Stanislawa Leszczynska delivered 3,000 babies at the concentration camp, too. But many of these children did not survive the camp.

Gates of Auschwitz

Prisoners who had special talents sometimes escaped execution by working for the Nazis.

PEOPLE TO KNOW **FANIA FÉNELON** was born Fanny Goldstein. Her father was Jewish and her mother was Catholic. But the Nazis considered her Jewish and sent her to the Birkenau concentration camp. The former club singer survived by volunteering to sing for the Birkenau Women's Orchestra to entertain the Nazis.

PEOPLE TO KNOW **JANINA IWANSKA** was 14 years old when she was shipped to Auschwitz. She slept in the children's bunkhouse and took care of the younger prisoners. This effort saved her from Nazi execution.

Janina Iwanska

Escapes and Deaths

- Most Jews who survived did so by working for the Nazis or hiding. But some adopted new identities and hid in plain sight. They were called the "Invisibles."

- The Invisibles bounced from hiding place to hiding place, sometimes sleeping in places such as movie theaters to remain unseen. Some survived to tell their stories. Some were lost to the war.

PERSON TO KNOW **HANNI WEISSENBERG** was 17 years old when the Gestapo pounded on her apartment door in Berlin, Germany, in 1943. She snuck out of the apartment window, dyed her hair blond, and became Hannelore Winkler, a girl the Nazis wouldn't hate. She lived to age 95.

Ideal Nazi girl on propaganda poster

◆ Many people imprisoned in concentration camps died of starvation and disease. They were supposed to get soup for lunch and dinner with one piece of bread. But Nazi guards often stole the prisoners' food rations.

◆ Concentration camps were often called "work camps" because the prisoners were forced into hard labor. They had to break rocks with shovels, build roads and equipment, and even dig trenches with their bare hands.

Poisonous-gas chambers became the most infamous method of execution in concentration camps.

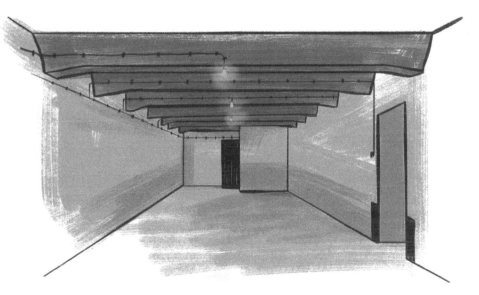

Gas chamber

CHAPTER 5

ALLIES VS. AXIS
(1939-1945)

Once the Allied powers declared war against the Axis powers, the fighting was brutal and intense. The Axis were trying to reshape the world into a place where self-centered leaders made the rules, and the people obeyed or paid the price for disobedience. The Allies were fighting to resist Axis domination. The side with the strongest weapons and the biggest armies would likely be victorious. Only the Axis powers had worked to rebuild their military forces after World War I, so the Allies were in real danger of being defeated.

- **The United States believed in democracy but refused to join the Allied powers at first. Americans were sick of war.**

- **France and Great Britain had no choice when it came to fighting Hitler and the Nazis because they had to defend their borders.**

- **Some European countries, like Denmark and Norway, tried to remain neutral, but Hitler made that impossible when he invaded them.**

Medics

Medics helped wounded soldiers on the battlefield. Most Allied forces tried not to hurt medics on either side.

Medic helmet

Some Axis forces used wounded soldiers as bait. When Allied medics tried to help the injured men, the medics were killed.

Not all Allied soldiers were compassionate and not all Axis soldiers were cruel. Calculating risk was very difficult.

Famous European Battles and Leaders

PEOPLE TO KNOW **COMMANDER WOLFRAM VON RICHTHOFEN** led the first battle of World War II and six more major air campaigns from 1936 to 1944. He was Hitler's senior air commander.

▶ Nazis bombed the town of Wieluń, Poland, at 4:40 a.m. on September 1, 1939. There were no military targets, only civilians.

Ruins of Wielun

STAT FACT Nearly **400 BOMBS** destroyed **75 PERCENT** of the city of Wieluń.

▶ Germany invaded Norway by sea on April 9, 1940. The Nazis set up a new government and removed anti-Nazi leadership.

TERM TO KNOW The French built concrete domes on their borders. This defensive wall was called the **MAGINOT LINE**.

◆ In 1870, France lost the Battle of Sedan to Germany. German Panzer tanks were too strong for the Maginot Line, and they rolled past the barriers. France fell a short time later.

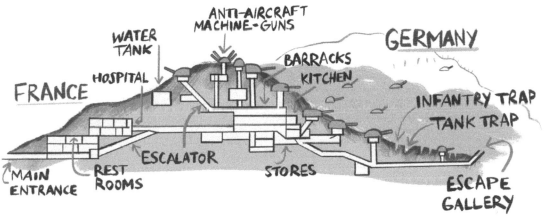

Maginot Line

▤ The English Channel was Britain's best line of defense. This stretch of water was all that stood between them and Hitler.

◆ British fighter planes defeated German bomber planes in the Battle of Britain in October 1940.

North African Battles and Leaders

▤ Hitler wanted control of North Africa because the northern coast was rich in oil. War machines require oil to function.

PEOPLE TO KNOW Nazi field marshal **ERWIN ROMMEL** was called the "Desert Fox." He was known for daring battles in the unforgiving sands of the Middle East.

▤ Rommel called his troops the **AFRIKA KORPS**.

➡ Operation Compass was the first major operation of World War II in North Africa. Allied forces successfully defeated Italian forces in Egypt and Libya from December 1940 to February 1941.

➡ Dust storms and water shortages made it hard for soldiers to manage the North African deserts they were trying to claim.

The bites of tsetse flies and mosquitos spread disease among soldiers.

⭐ The Second Battle of El Alamein began on October 23, 1942. During the conflict, New Zealand soldiers turned North Africa in favor of the Allies.

STAT FACT Nearly **10,000** New Zealanders died and more than **4,000** became prisoners of war after the Second Battle of El Alamein. But they still defeated the Nazis.

Famous Mediterranean Battles and Leaders

When World War II started, Britain ruled the island of Malta in the Mediterranean Sea near Italy. They considered giving Malta to Italian dictator Mussolini as a bribe not to join Hitler.

Italy joined the Axis powers in 1940. Great Britain saw Malta as an important location to fight Mussolini.

⭐ Britain had to convince the people of Malta they were willing to defend them against Italy. They rebuilt 1934 biplanes called Gloster Gladiators to fly missions over the island. The plans were named Faith, Hope, and Charity.

Gloster Gladiator

Most of Mussolini's Italian ships were anchored in the port of Taranto. The British set out to disable the ships.

STAT FACT On November 11, 1940, **19** British biplanes known as Fairey Swordfishes flew to Taranto. They were old planes from World War I, but they still damaged **THREE** battleships and killed nearly **700** Italian seamen in the mission called Operation Judgement. Mussolini never attacked the British Navy after this defeat.

★ Patrol torpedo boats, known as PT boats, helped win battles in the Mediterranean Sea on the coasts of Italy, Algeria, and North Africa.

PT boat

Japan Attacks China

→ The invasion of Poland in 1939 is usually marked as the beginning of World War II. But some say it actually started when Japan attacked Manchuria, China, in 1931 to exploit their natural resources.

PERSON TO KNOW **CHIANG KAI-SHEK** was the leader of the Chinese Nationalist government. By 1937, he had moved to inland China to escape Japan's attack on coastal cities, including Shanghai, Beijing, and Nanjing.

STAT FACT Between 1931 and 1945, Japanese soldiers killed **20 MILLION** Chinese people, most of them civilians.

TERM TO KNOW **KAMIKAZES** were Japanese fighter pilots who were directed to sacrifice their lives by purposely crashing their planes into targets. *Kamikaze* means "divine wind" in Japanese.

Kamikaze pilots

➤ Japan employed their first kamikaze pilots on October 25, 1944, during the Battle of the Leyte Gulf in the Philippines. The young Japanese pilots were supposed to disable American warships by diving their bomb-loaded airplanes into the decks.

PERSON TO KNOW Japanese naval captain **MOTOHARU OKAMURA** said, "I firmly believe that the only way to swing the war in our favor is to resort to crash-dive attacks with our planes."

CHAPTER 6

JAPAN ATTACKS AMERICA
(1941)

The United States resisted joining the Allies during World War II. The battles were so far away, and it wasn't really America's fight. The United States also had its own problems. The Great Depression had left millions out of work, and the country was still recovering from World War I. Most Americans wanted the Allies to win World War II, so the country provided military equipment to strengthen Allied defenses. But it wasn't until Japan attacked a US naval base in Hawaii that the war overseas hit American territory. That strike brought America into the fight.

- ➤ **Pearl Harbor was the most important American naval base in the Pacific Ocean.**

- ➤ **American military leaders in Hawaii called the Pacific Ocean "vacant." They didn't expect the enemy approaching from across the vast waters.**

- ➤ **Radar technology was new during World War II. Radar operators at Pearl Harbor could detect some aircraft, but missed others.**

Lead-up to the Attack

◆ Army Privates George Elliot and Joe Lockard were nearly finished with their shift monitoring mobile radar on the island of Oahu when they spotted a spike at 7:00 a.m. on December 7, 1941. At least 50 planes were headed their way.

◆ A group of B-17 bomber planes headed for Hawaii was spotted on the radar. Lieutenant Kermit Tyler thought they were US planes. He said, "Don't worry about it."

The radar had detected a swarm of Japanese aircraft, not US planes. The Americans were not prepared.

Mobile radar

Attack on Pearl Harbor

◆ Japan understood that the only way to beat America was to destroy their navy. Pearl Harbor was the logical place to start. After months of planning, they struck on the morning of December 7.

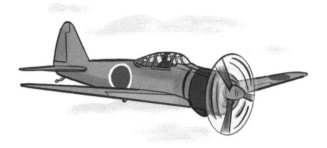

Japanese fighter plane used at Pearl Harbor

STAT FACT **FOUR** Japanese aircraft carriers launched 353 Japanese aircraft in the Pacific Ocean. They hit Pearl Harbor in two waves, using **40** torpedo planes, **103** bomber planes, **131** dive-bombers, and **79** fighter planes.

PERSON TO KNOW The Japanese aircraft were commanded by **ADMIRAL ISOROKU YAMAMOTO**. He had originally opposed Japan's alliance with Germany as well as the invasion of China and war with the United States.

STAT FACT In just **TWO** hours, **2,403** United States soldiers and civilians were killed by Japanese pilots. **NINETEEN** US naval ships, including **EIGHT** battleships, were damaged or destroyed.

▶ The USS *Arizona* was a battleship that had returned to its base at Pearl Harbor the day before the attack. It suffered the most damage and greatest loss of life. After it was struck and exploded, it sank to the bottom of the ocean and took 1,117 lives with it.

Attack on Pearl Harbor

★ Three US aircraft carriers that would have been hit were spared because they were away at sea practicing military exercises.

America's Reaction

President Franklin D. Roosevelt called December 7, the day of the Pearl Harbor attack, "a date which will live in infamy."

Japan had attacked Malaya, later part of Malaysia, the day before Pearl Harbor. Hong Kong, Guam, the Philippines, Wake Island, and Midway Island were also attacked on December 7.

⭐ Production of military equipment ramped up in the wake of Pearl Harbor. Trucks, jeeps, tanks, artillery, heavy bombers, fighter planes, ships, and amphibious vehicles were produced at a rate the world had never seen.

PERSON TO KNOW First Lady **ELEANOR ROOSEVELT** asked Americans to help one another. "When we find a way to do anything more in our communities to help others, to build morale, or to give a feeling of security," she said, "we must do it."

Eleanor Roosevelt with American troops

★ Before the United States joined World War II, some young men were barred from military service because of bad teeth. These standards were changed to allow more men to join the force.

◆ Americans were divided on many issues, but they came together to fight a common enemy and win World War II.

Declarations of War

In June 1941, Hitler turned on his Soviet partners by attacking their city of Stalingrad during Operation Barbarossa.

▸ When Stalin realized Hitler had broken the German-Soviet Nonaggression Pact by attacking Stalingrad, he declared war on Germany and joined forces with the Allies in October 1941.

▸ President Roosevelt went to the US Congress to get permission to declare war on Japan. The vote went in his favor and war was declared on December 8, 1941.

Roosevelt addresses Congress

★ Japan didn't officially declare war on the United States and Great Britain until two hours after the Pearl Harbor attack. They had planned to make the declaration 30 minutes before the attack, but it took too long to deliver the message.

♦ Germany declared war on the United States on December 11, 1941, at 3:30 p.m. (Berlin time). Some of Hitler's advisers were against it, but Hitler was sure Japan would defeat America.

The United States of America declared war on Germany on December 12, 1941.

Recruitment and the Draft

Draftee undergoing a medical exam

◆ The Selective Training and Service Act of 1940 was also known as the draft or conscription. It required all men between 21 and 35 years of age to register for possible military service. Those selected were required to fight.

STAT FACT In 1939, the United States Army had **174,000** soldiers, including the Air Force. That number grew to **8 MILLION** in 1940. Another **3.4 MILLION** joined the Navy.

Roughly 39 percent of US soldiers had volunteered to serve their country. They left their jobs to help the Allies win World War II.

⭐ After the attack on Pearl Harbor, the draft expanded to include all men between the ages of 18 and 65. It remained so until March 1947.

STAT FACT Women were not included in the draft, but **350,000** women served in the American military during World War II. They held positions in the Women's Army Corp, the Women's Airforce Service Pilots, and the Women Accepted for Volunteer Emergency Service. They also served in the Marines and the Coast Guard.

➡ Most women who served in the military had office jobs as typists, clerks, or mail sorters. But some women, especially those working in medical services, saw battle.

Women's Airforce Service Pilots

Life in the Military

New military recruits were required to attend basic training, also known as "boot camp."

In boot camp, new soldiers learned to work as part of a team. Together, they could accomplish important missions they couldn't possibly tackle alone. That cooperation might save their lives in battle.

⭐ **One way to remind the recruits they were part of a team was through haircuts and uniforms. Shaved heads made most new soldiers look like brothers. They also ate, slept, and trained together in order to form strong relationships.**

Would-be soldiers waiting outside a recruiting station

◆ Soldiers learned to kill the enemy before the enemy could kill them. But killing didn't make them killers. Seeing so much death made them value life even more.

▤ Every soldier at every rank had an important role to play when bullets and bombs threatened lives.

PERSON TO KNOW Cartoonist **BILL MAULDIN** joined the Army when he was 19. He quickly began to capture the real world of the men trying to survive during World War II.

Bill Mauldin

The African-American Experience

STAT FACT In 1941, fewer than **4,000** African Americans were allowed to enlist in the US Army. Only **12** became officers. Four years later, **1.2 MILLION** African Americans were in active service.

➡ African American soldiers were segregated from white soldiers. They were confined to separate sleeping quarters, dining halls, recreation centers, and hospital wards, and there were blood banks for Black soldiers only.

African American soldiers who became officers could only command Black soldiers.

PERSON TO KNOW **VERNON BAKER** was born in 1919, just 54 years after slavery was abolished in the United States. He became an officer and later won the Medal of Honor—but he wasn't granted the medal until 1996, 50 years after he served.

PERSON TO KNOW Only about 1,000 African Americans in the US Army Air Force became pilots. **LEE ARCHER JR.** was one of them. As a Tuskegee Airman, he escorted US bomber planes over Europe. He even flew three successful missions in a single day.

Lee Archer Jr., Tuskegee Airmen pilot

⭐ The *Booker T. Washington* was a type of US cargo ship called a Liberty ship. It was named for Black educator Booker T. Washington and christened by Marian Anderson, a famous Black opera singer.

The Japanese-American Experience

★ American-born citizens whose parents immigrated from Japan are known as Nisei. In November 1941, the Army set up a secret language school that trained Nisei to be interpreters.

PERSON TO KNOW **DANIEL INOUYE** was Nisei and born in Hawaii. When Japan attacked his home, he wanted to join the Army, but Japanese Americans weren't allowed to enlist because of a racist rule. Later, the rule changed. Inouye enlisted and became an American hero. After the war, he represented Hawaii in the US Senate for 53 years.

➡ More than 19,000 Japanese Americans served in the 100th Infantry Battalion, 442nd Regimental Combat Team and Military Intelligence Service. It became the most decorated US military unit in history.

Members of the 442nd Regimental Combat Team

◆ When President Roosevelt signed Executive Order 9066, he launched a deeply shameful period in American history. From 1942 to 1945, Japanese Americans were forced into internment camps.

TERM TO KNOW **INTERNMENT CAMPS** were guarded prisons where Japanese Americans lived in isolation under the harshest conditions. These prisoners had committed no crimes.

Woman and child in an internment camp

◆ When Japanese Americans were forced from their homes, they were permitted to carry one suitcase of belongings. Everything else they owned, including their homes and businesses, was sold or given away by the US government. They received no compensation.

CHAPTER 7

ON THE US HOMEFRONT
(1940-1945)

When America entered World War II, citizens were asked to help with the war effort. President Roosevelt called this collective action the "Arsenal of Democracy." It was suddenly essential to build a bigger, stronger military force. This effort required millions of new soldiers and military machines. But it also required new people to cover soldiers' jobs after they left to fight the war. Extra metal, extra fabric, extra rubber, extra food, extra *everything* would be necessary to meet the challenges of war. People at home had to manage with less. Under Roosevelt's leadership, Americans met the challenge.

- President Roosevelt's peacetime draft of new soldiers became critical with the United States at war.

- American men between the ages of 18 and 64 were required to register for the draft. Thirty-six million men registered.

- Serving the country as a soldier was seen as patriotic.

Uniform Duty

➡ Soldiers needed uniforms, and American factories had to make them. Each soldier was given a metal helmet, a shirt, a sweatshirt, trousers, socks, boots, an ammo belt, a canteen, a gas mask, a rifle, an armband, dog tags, and special patches.

STAT FACT Wool was used to make soldiers' uniforms. Every soldier required at least **75 POUNDS** of wool for their uniforms each year.

⭐ Soldiers wore M1 helmets with an outer shell of steel, plastic lining, and a canvas chin strap. The helmet weighed 2.85 pounds.

Factory Fixes

TERM TO KNOW In January 1943, President Roosevelt established the **WAR PRODUCTION BOARD** to convert existing American factories into factories for military supplies.

◆ Factories that made ordinary items quickly adapted to producing supplies for the troops. In 1943, the Maytag factory in Iowa stopped making washing machines and started making parts for warplanes.

★ The Lionel factory, which made toy trains, started producing compasses for warships.

Lionel toy trains

The Mattatuck Manufacturing factory made upholstery nails for furniture before the war. After Pearl Harbor, they made ammunition clips for Springfield rifles.

The Ford Motor Company produced B-24 Liberator bomber planes.

B-24 Liberator bomber

STAT FACT In 1941, American factories produced **3 MILLION** automobiles. But during World War II, only **139** were made. The factories made trucks, tanks, airplane engines, and guns instead.

Work for Women

With so many men fighting the war in Europe and the Pacific, factories had to depend on a brand-new workforce: women. A poster campaign showing "Rosie the Riveter" encouraged women to work.

STAT FACT In 1940, only **27 PERCENT** of American women worked outside the home. By 1945, it had grown to **37 PERCENT**. One out of every four married women worked outside the home for the war effort.

With fathers fighting the war and more mothers working outside the home, children had fewer caretakers. Women received grants from the government to pay the cost of child care.

Rosie the Riveter

★ First Lady Eleanor Roosevelt was so impressed to discover women could join the military in Great Britain, she asked US General George Marshall to create a woman's service branch in the army.

➡ In May 1942, the Women's Auxiliary Army Corps was created. When the name changed to the Women's Army Corps, the female soldiers were known as WACs. They worked in the United States, in Europe, and on the Pacific war front.

★ More than 350,000 women became soldiers, including hundreds who became Women's Airforce Service Pilots. The pilots were awarded the Congressional Gold Medal in 2010.

All Americans Joined the Fight

➧ Before World War II, many African Americans were banned from high-paying jobs. President Roosevelt created the National Defense Advisory Commission in June of 1940 to address these racist hiring policies.

Anti-discrimination policies looked good on paper, but progress was slow. White Americans were resistant to racial fairness in the workplace.

GROUP TO KNOW THE NATIONAL ASSOCIATION FOR THE ADVANCEMENT OF COLORED PEOPLE (NAACP) is a civil rights organization that works to end racial injustice. In 1941 the NAACP said they planned to march on Washington to draw attention to the government's unfair hiring practices. This made President Roosevelt act.

Black protesters against racist hiring policies

In response to the NAACP's planned protest, President Roosevelt signed Executive Order 8802 in 1941. It forbade racial discrimination in government hiring and training programs. This order didn't solve the problem, but it was a step in the right direction.

STAT FACT After 1941, **1 MILLION** African Americans finally found employment. About **600,000** of them were Black women.

⭐ White female factory workers were sometimes called "Rosie the Riveters." They appeared on magazine covers and political posters. But there were proud Black Rosies, too. They were underrepresented in the news but worked equally hard.

Doing Without

As America's resources were diverted to the war effort, production of day-to-day supplies began to slow.

◆ President Roosevelt created a system of rationing. Certain goods that had to be sent overseas for the war effort were rationed at home. Each citizen was allowed a limited amount of these items.

◆ Rationed goods included cars, tires, gasoline, oil, firewood, nylon, silk, shoes, meat, coffee, sugar, jelly, canned milk, and lard.

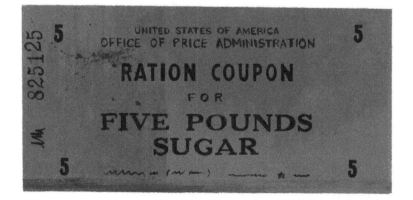

★ British soldiers had to ration their toilet paper. They were limited to three sheets per day. American soldiers were allowed 22 sheets each day.

◆ The Office of Price Administration was created to set the amount of rationed goods each citizen could buy. It also controlled prices.

★ "Do with less, so they'll have enough" became a rallying cry and a sign of American patriotism. Using less at home meant soldiers would have what they needed to fight.

★ Posters popped up across the country to celebrate the spirit of sharing the load. Giving things up made Americans feel more connected to the soldiers fighting far away. It also inspired new soldiers to join the fight.

Recycling for Uncle Sam

★ Recycling became a way of life during World War II. Materials like copper were recycled to create electrical wiring. Copper pennies were melted down and recycled. New pennies were made of steel instead.

Steel pennies

◆ Scrap metal was recycled for military machines. Pots and pans, metal toys, car fenders, chain link fences, and even old Civil War cannons were melted down and donated to the war effort.

★ Old music records were recycled to create new recordings of music made especially for the troops. The project was called Records for Our Fighting Men.

STAT FACT When the war effort needed rubber, the government held a rubber drive. People turned in **450,000 TONS** of old tires, hot water bottles, raincoats, rainboots, and floor mats.

→ People recycled cans by washing them and leaving them in boxes by the curb. Boy Scouts gathered the boxes and delivered them to neighborhood collection sites.

★ Paper was in short supply during World War II. Most lumber workers were at war, and the few who remained couldn't keep up with the demand. Recycling existing paper helped ease the shortage.

Posters encouraged recycling

Valiant Volunteers

In February 1941, the Red Cross launched a blood drive for wounded soldiers. When Japan attacked Pearl Harbor 10 months later, the mission became more important than ever.

STAT FACT By 1945, **7.5 MILLION** Red Cross volunteers and **39,000** paid staffers served **16 MILLION** troops and **1 MILLION** war casualties. American citizens donated **$784 MILLION** to support the Red Cross during the war.

⭐ The Red Cross provided more than medical help. Its club services provided meals and recreational activities for overseas soldiers to lighten the burden of war.

Red Cross Clubmobile giving out doughnuts

★ The Red Cross Clubmobile was equipped with a kitchen and a doughnut machine. Women who volunteered for Clubmobiles made coffee and doughnuts for the troops. They were called "Donut Dollies."

Knit for Defense was a program for volunteers to knit vests, socks, sweaters, and scarves for soldiers abroad.

➡ The Ground Observer Corps was a volunteer effort to protect America from attacks on the homeland. Teenagers, housewives, and the elderly used binoculars to watch the sea and the sky for signs of enemy planes, ships, and submarines.

Even Eleanor Roosevelt joined the Knit for Defense program.

Paying for the War

World War II was very expensive. If it was financed today, it would cost **$4.1 TRILLION**.

STAT FACT America increased taxes to help pay for the war. In 1940, before World War II, only 7 percent of American citizens were required to pay income taxes. By 1944, 64 percent of the population paid tax on their earnings.

→ The wealthiest Americans were taxed 94 percent of their income in 1944 and 1945. This tax rate applied to people making $200,000 and above, what would be about $2.9 million today.

War drained US treasury reserves

⭐ The United States spent a fortune on the war but cut corners in other ways. One law banned the government from spending more than $750 on a single automobile, including the president's guarded vehicle.

◆ Citizens were encouraged to buy war bonds from the government. These bonds were official-looking certificates that would increase in value over time.

War bonds

STAT FACT More than **85 MILLION** Americans bought war bonds and raised **$185.7 BILLION** for the war.

Celebrity Soldiers

PERSON TO KNOW Some Hollywood actors signed up to serve their country during World War II. **JIMMY STEWART**, star of the classic Christmas movie *It's a Wonderful Life*, joined the Army Air Corp as a B-24 pilot. He flew 20 combat missions over Germany and France.

PERSON TO KNOW **CLARK GABLE**, star of the film *Gone with the Wind*, volunteered for the air force. He spent weeks in Officer Candidate School, where he learned to be an aerial gunner.

Clark Gable

PERSON TO KNOW Before **RONALD REAGAN** was president, he was a Hollywood actor. He also served in the air force during World War II.

PERSON TO KNOW **SIR ALEC GUINNESS** joined the British Royal Navy in 1939. He invaded the coast of Italy with 200 fellow British soldiers in July 1943. He later became a famous actor and played Obi-Wan Kenobi in the original *Star Wars* films.

PERSON TO KNOW Silent film star **CHARLIE CHAPLIN** didn't serve in the military, but he did join the fight against Hitler by creating a movie in 1940 called *The Great Dictator*. It helped Americans understand how dangerous the real dictator actually was.

Charlie Chaplin

PERSON TO KNOW Actor and dancer **GENE KELLY** enlisted in the navy during World War II. He made training films for the military.

Food Facts

⭐ Food rationing began in 1940, almost a year before America entered the war. Each person was limited to one egg, four ounces of butter, and eight ounces of sugar each week.

Weekly food ration

➡ Sugar was in short supply because Japan was at war in the Philippines. Cargo ships that normally imported sugar were diverted, so the national supply of sugar dropped by more than a third.

GROUP TO KNOW The **AMERICAN FAT SALVAGE COMMITTEE** asked people to save the fat left over from cooking rationed bacon. Fat was used to make glycerin, and glycerin was used to make bombs.

★ A Disney public service film starring Minnie Mouse claimed "every year 2 billion pounds of waste kitchen fats are thrown away—enough glycerin for 10 billion rapid-fire cannon shells."

In 1937 Hershey created a high-energy snack for soldiers that was designed to resist melting in high temperatures. It did not taste great.

Army ration chocolate

STAT FACT By 1943, **20 MILLION** families had planted **7 MILLION ACRES** of gardens, growing **15 BILLION POUNDS** of food. These "victory gardens" produced **40 PERCENT** of America's fresh vegetables.

CHAPTER 8

TOOLS OF WAR

By the end of World War I, most global military supplies had dwindled. Though the Allies defeated the Central Powers, they would need more weapons for the next war. When Hitler rose to power, he rushed to develop dangerous technologies. The Allies feared their old tools might not be adequate for fighting the new war. Some of the old machinery was used, like faded hand-me-down clothing. But new weapons were emerging on the land, in the air, and on the seas. Both sides spent millions and millions of dollars on armament. The warriors with the best weapons were destined to win World War II.

- **The Treaty of Versailles forbade Germany from developing new armies or weapons. But Hitler broke the rules almost immediately.**

- **Almost all world powers asked their scientists to create new weapons that would give them the military edge.**

- **Even today, new ways to kill are being tested and developed for any future wars.**

Hand-Me-Downs

★ Biplanes made of wood and canvas are seen as World War I relics. But Great Britain, France, the Soviet Union, and Italy used these faithful standbys during World War II.

◆ Italy's Beretta semi-automatic service pistol was launched in 1915. It was used through World War I and World War II, with some improvements added in 1919 and 1923.

◆ The Mk 2 grenade was an explosive device used in World War I and World War II. It was called a "pineapple" grenade because it had grooves in its shell that made it look like a pineapple. These grooves were supposed to make it easier to grip.

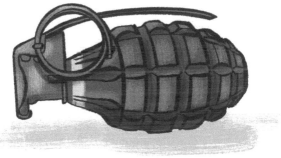

Mk 2 grenade

Weapons in the Air

STAT FACT America's Boeing B-17 bomber was almost **75 FEET** long, weighed **65,000 POUNDS**, and had a wingspan of almost **104 FEET**. The aircraft carried **11 TO 13** machine guns and nearly **10,000 POUNDS** of explosives. It held a 10-man crew: two pilots, a bombardier, a navigator, a radio operator, and five gunners.

➡ The Messerschmitt Bf 109 was the Luftwaffe's best fighter plane. More than 33,000 of these fast, agile, high-altitude machines flew all over Europe during World War II.

The Supermarine Spitfire and the Hawker Hurricane helped the British defeat German pilots in aerial duels during the Battle of Britain in 1940.

British Hawker Hurricane planes

Germany's Arado AR 196 was a two-person float plane. Launched from ships using a catapult, it had a cannon on each wing, a machine gun in its nose, and one or two guns in the second cockpit. It also carried a 110-pound bomb under each wing.

Arado AR 196

Japan's Mitsubishi A6M Zero was called "invincible." It was one of the most agile airplanes ever built.

★ The American P-51 Mustang was a deadly dogfighter. More than 281 American pilots earned "ace" status in Mustangs by each taking five enemy planes out of the skies.

Ships at Sea

★ The *Bismarck* was Germany's first new battleship since World War I. After eight days of battle with British warships, it sank in the North Atlantic.

➡ Japan's *Yamato* was one of two of the biggest battleships in the world. It was **863 FEET** long and weighed nearly **73,000 TONS**. With **NINE 18-INCH** guns and **101** smaller guns, it launched **SEVEN** aircraft. *Yamato* sank on April 7, 1945, along with **2,498** of its men.

Yamato

The USS *Iowa* was **887 FEET** long and weighed **45,000 TONS**. When the war ended, it brought American prisoners of war home from Japan.

On November 12, 1943, President Roosevelt boarded the USS *Iowa* for North Africa, where he had a meeting with Churchill and Stalin.

The mascot of the USS *Iowa* was a dog named Vicky. She wasn't the only seagoing animal. Minnie was the prized tabby cat on the HMS *Argonaut*. The whole ship was her home, even as it invaded Normandy on D-Day.

Vicky, the mascot of the USS *Iowa*

The *Nea Hellas* was a British training ship during World War II. A canary named Jib joined the crew in November 1943. She sang on the open deck and lifted the crew's spirits.

Rolling Thunder

The US military needed a beefy road transport. It turned out to be the jeep. This army workhorse was light but rugged.

→ Three companies competed to make a road vehicle for the military. American Bantam Car Company proposed the Blitz Buggy, Willy's Overland Motors proposed Willy's Quad, and Ford Motor Company proposed the Ford Pygmy. In the end, Willy's Overland Motors created the iconic jeep.

★ Soldiers nicknamed the jeep "Eugene." The name came from a cartoon dog in the comic strip *Popeye*.

"Eugene" the Jeep

⭐ America's M4A3E8 Sherman Tank was feared on the European battlefield because it had a bigger, more powerful engine than the original Sherman Tank. Its thicker armor and wider tracks made it easy to master any terrain.

The Tiger II was a German tank that was practically unstoppable. Tank ace Kurt Knispel made 168 kills in his Tiger II.

Tiger II

◆ Great Britain eventually introduced a tank of their own. The Comet was a last-minute champion during the close of the war. It had a huge cannon, a Rolls-Royce Meteor engine, and bomb-busting armor.

Guns, Guns, Guns

➡ The M2 Browning .50 caliber machine gun was introduced in 1918. It was too late to help in the trenches of World War I, but it was successful in the Second World War and is still used today.

▤ The semi-automatic M1 Garand rifle could fire clips of eight bullets as fast as a soldier could pull the trigger.

★ The M1 Thompson submachine gun, nicknamed the "Tommy gun," was the favorite weapon of gangsters in the 1920s. It was also used by American soldiers in World War II.

"Tommy gun"

★ Some people might call the M101 Howitzer a gun, but it's more like a cannon on wheels. The huge shells could take out a building or a tank.

M101 Howitzer

◆ The Bazooka was a shoulder-mounted cannon that could fire an explosive shell from a safe distance. General Dwight D. Eisenhower called the bazooka, the atom bomb, and the jeep "tools of victory."

STAT FACT The K98 Mauser rifle was a favorite among German snipers. It weighed just **EIGHT POUNDS** without a scope, was only **43.5 INCHES** long, and could fire **FIVE** rounds with great accuracy.

Chemical Weapons

➤ Hitler's chemists developed **SARIN GAS**. It attacks the nervous system, causing the loss of consciousness, convulsions, and death. Even Hitler knew it would be too dangerous to use in combat.

➤ German bombers dropped explosives on the coastal town of Bari, Italy, in 1943. Dozens of Allied ships were in flames, and hundreds of people developed a mystery illness. Mustard gas had been released, but not by the Germans. It was stockpiled in an Allied ship bombed by the Nazis.

➤ The Imperial Japanese Army left 700,000 bombs and drums of mustard gas and lewisite gas behind when they left China in 1945. Both nations are still trying to clean it up—even today.

Soldier wearing a gas mask

★ During World War I, Winston Churchill said, "Gas is a more merciful weapon than the high explosive shell and compels the enemy to accept a decision with less loss of life." He suggested using gas in World War II but was overruled.

◆ During World War II, the US Army tested mustard gas and lewisite on 60,000 white, Japanese American, African American, and Puerto Rican soldiers while they were locked in a wooden chamber. This racist experiment attempted to test whether the soldiers reacted differently to the gas.

Adolf Hitler was temporarily blinded by British chemical gas when he fought in World War I.

Soldier inspecting mustard gas canisters

CHAPTER 9

SPIES AND SECRET CODES

Many people fought on battlefields during World War II, but they weren't the only ones working to defeat the enemy. Others helped in secret. Nearly every nation involved in the war had experts trained in espionage, the art of spying. Some spies simply carried messages, while others dug up information that would change the course of the war. Both men and women spied. There were spies of every age, culture, and race. Some lost their lives trying to serve their countries undercover. All had remarkable stories to tell.

➤ **The Office of Strategic Services (OSS) was formed to supervise US spies in 1942. It later became the Central Intelligence Agency (CIA).**

➤ **Great Britain's spy team was the Special Operations Executive (SOE). It had more than 13,000 men and women in its service during the war.**

➤ **The Abwehr was the intelligence agency for German spies. But the Nazis Sicherheitsdienst des Reichsführers (SD) was in competition with the Abwehr.**

Navajo Code Talkers

➤ When Japan broke American coded messages with ease, the US Army recruited soldiers from the Indigenous Navajo Nation to create code from a language the Japanese could not translate.

STAT FACT Approximately **400** Navajo men made the Code Talkers team a remarkable success.

⭐ In 1982, President Ronald Reagan proclaimed that August 14 was National Navajo Code Talkers Day to celebrate the Navajo specialists. In 2001, President George W. Bush honored 29 Navajo Code Talkers with a specially designed bronze medal for their skilled service.

Code Talkers

Code Makers

TERM TO KNOW **CRYPTOLOGY** is the study of decoding. Codes helped both sides keep their messages confidential during World War II—as long as they weren't decoded by the enemy.

➡ The German military used a machine called the Enigma. It used mathematical code to send low-level secret messages by air and sea. The Germans shared the Enigma with their Japanese allies.

Enigma

★ After 1940, Hitler used the Lorenz cipher machine to send top-secret messages to his generals. It was more advanced and faster than the Enigma.

★ Codes have been used in politics and war for thousands of years. Julius Caesar used a code to keep his messages secret when he became the Roman dictator in 49 BCE. The code became known as the Caesar cipher.

◆ The Greek Spartan military used a simple machine called a scytale cipher to code their secret messages. A letter-stamped ribbon wrapped around a cylinder would reveal the message, but only if the cylinder was the right size.

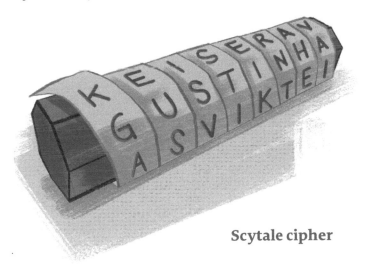

Scytale cipher

★ The pigpen cipher was used by a group called the Freemasons to keep their files secret. It replaces each letter with a geometric shape.

Code Breakers

◆ For every group creating a code during World War II, there was another group trying to break it. Great Britain established the Government Code and Cypher School at an estate known as Bletchley Park.

PERSON TO KNOW One of the most legendary code breakers was Captain **JERRY ROBERTS**. He and his team at Bletchley Park broke Hitler's Lorenz cipher and turned the tide for the Allies during World War II.

★ Mathematician Bill Tutte figured out how the Lorenz cipher worked without ever seeing the machine.

A team of Polish mathematicians led by Marian Rejewski began breaking the Enigma code in the 1930s. When Germany invaded Poland, they turned their research over to the British.

PERSON TO KNOW **ALAN TURING** was an English mathematician and pioneer in the field of computer science. His group at Bletchley Park cracked the Enigma code in 1943. Thousands of secret messages sent by the Germans and Japanese were decoded.

Alan Turing was commemorated on Great Britain's 50-pound note on June 23, 2021.

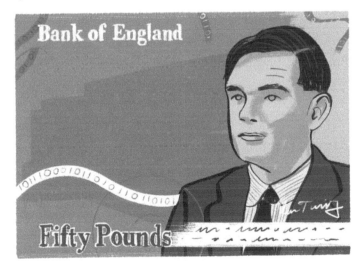

Alan Turing on the British pound

Spy Gear

◆ The coal grenade was invented during the US Civil War. Confederate spies made the explosive look like a piece of coal and hid it in Union coal supplies. The fake coal blew up when it was placed in fire. The American OSS and British SOE re-created the this weapon during World War II.

★ When spies were captured and imprisoned by the Germans, the British OSS sent them escape maps disguised as Monopoly games and playing cards.

★ The OSS developed an underwater breathing aid for spies. The device was called SCUBA, but it's not the same scuba gear divers use today.

★ The British SOE introduced rodent bombs during World War II. Dead rat bodies filled with explosives were scattered across enemy factory floors. When unsuspecting soldiers tossed the rats into fire, they ignited.

★ In 1942, American secret agents planned to lace goat feces with a poison called anthrax. They wanted to plant it in Nazi camps to take down enemy soldiers. The stinky idea was abandoned.

★ The British SOE planned to launch the pipe pistol, a gun disguised as a tobacco pipe. It was never put into actual use.

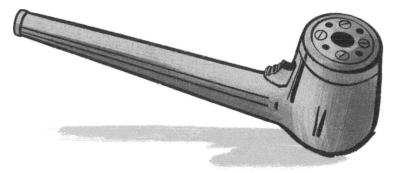

Pipe pistol prototype

Famous Female Spies

PERSON TO KNOW **JULIA CHILD**
is famous for her cookbooks
and cooking show. But before
she worked on recipes, she
worked on secret formulas for
the OSS.

Julia Child

PERSON TO KNOW When **VIOLETTE SZABO**'s husband, Etienne, was killed by the Nazis, she wanted to fight back. The 23-year-old joined the British SOE as a spy. She was captured in France and sent to the Ravensbrück concentration camp. She tried to escape but was executed hours before Russian Allies liberated the camp.

PERSON TO KNOW **VIRGINIA HALL** was an American spy with one prosthetic leg. She became the most highly decorated female spy during World War II.

PERSON TO KNOW **NANCY WAKE** was born in New Zealand and moved to England when she was 16. During the war, she spied for the SOE, a secret British intelligence agency. She was nicknamed "the White Mouse" because she escaped every Nazi trap.

PERSON TO KNOW **VELVALEE DICKINSON** owned a shop in New York. She sold dolls, but she also sold secrets to the Japanese government. She was jailed in 1944 and remained imprisoned until 1951.

PERSON TO KNOW **NOOR INAYAT KHAN** was born in Moscow to an Indian father and an American mother. She spied for the SOE in Nazi-occupied France before being captured and executed.

Noor Inayat Khan

Famous Male Spies

PERSON TO KNOW **EDDIE CHAPMAN** was a British double agent. He pretended to spy for the Nazis while actually spying for Great Britain.

PERSON TO KNOW **RICHARD SORGE** was a Soviet spy posing as a German journalist. He convinced his editor to send him to Japan, where he formed a Russian spy ring. The Japanese discovered his ploy and hanged him in 1944.

PERSON TO KNOW **JEAN-CLAUDE GUIET** was a freshman at Harvard when he was drafted in 1943. Within months, he was recruited by the OSS because he was fluent in French and English. Guiet became a spy and dropped into France by parachute.

Jean-Claude Guiet

PERSON TO KNOW **HANS-THILO SCHMIDT** worked at the German Armed Forces' Cipher Office. He sold secrets about the Enigma machine to the French.

PERSON TO KNOW As an SOE spy, **FOREST FREDERICK EDWARD YEO-THOMAS**, was captured, tortured, and imprisoned by the Gestapo repeatedly. But again and again he escaped while others were executed.

PERSON TO KNOW **ROALD DAHL** was a famous author of children's books, but before that he was an SOE spy. Great Britain needed to know if the United States might join the war, so Dahl socialized with American politicians and businessmen to gather information. He even charmed First Lady Eleanor Roosevelt.

Roald Dahl's RAF Airplane

People of the Resistance

PERSON TO KNOW **AUDREY HEPBURN** was a famous actress. As a child, she lived in the Netherlands when the Nazis occupied her country and killed her uncle. At age 15, she danced in ballet performances to raise money for the Dutch resistance.

PERSON TO KNOW **FREDDIE AND TRUUS OVERSTEEGEN** were teen sisters in Nazi-occupied Amsterdam. They worked for the Dutch resistance and even blew up Nazi trains.

→ In 1943, the Nazis planned to round up all the Jews in Denmark and take them to concentration camps. Hundreds of Danish fishermen carried 2,500 Jewish people by sea to safety in Sweden.

PERSON TO KNOW **ROBERT DE LA ROCHEFOUCAULD** was an SOE spy and a member of the French Resistance. He blew up Nazi factories and escaped Nazi concentration camps, living to tell his tale.

PERSON TO KNOW **JEAN MOULIN** was the first President of National Council of the Resistance, which oversaw the French Resistance. He was captured, tortured, and killed by the Gestapo.

PERSON TO KNOW **MARIE-MADELEINE FOURCADE** was a hero of the French Resistance. When Hitler invaded France, women were expected to stay silent. Fourcade rejected those expectations and came to lead the French Resistance with the code name "Hedgehog."

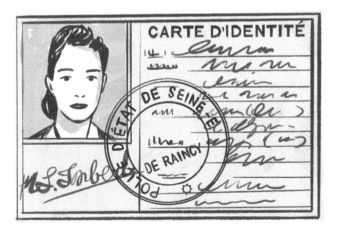

Marie-Madeleine Fourcade's ID card

People of the Resistance

◆ The Polish resistance provided more than half of the secret information that Allied forces gathered on the Nazis.

PERSON TO KNOW **WITOLD PILECKI** founded the Secret Polish Army after the Nazis occupied Poland. He allowed himself to be captured and sent to Auschwitz, then organized a resistance movement within the concentration camp.

PERSON TO KNOW **AUGUST BROWNE** was a jazz musician from Nigeria living in Poland when the Nazis invaded in 1939. He became the only Black member of the Polish resistance. Although 94 percent of Warsaw residents did not survive, Browne lived to tell his story.

August Browne

PERSON TO KNOW WILLIAM ALFRED EDDY was a Christian missionary in the Muslim world. When the United States joined the fight in World War II, his ability to speak Arabic made him an excellent spy for the OSS in North Africa.

PERSON TO KNOW MARCEL PINTE was only six years old when he carried messages for the French Resistance battling the Nazi occupation.

★ American intelligence officer FRANK MANUEL discovered Operation Werewolf. It was Hitler's secret plan to create a movement of loyal German citizens that would fight the Allies behind enemy lines with acts of vandalism and terrorism. The operation was a failure.

Operation Werewolf penant

CHAPTER 10

THE TIDE TURNS
(1944–1945)

Many see the Allied invasion of Nazi-occupied France as the turning point of World War II. But the beginning of Hitler's end started in 1941. As that year began, Hitler controlled most of Europe. Only Great Britain stood between him and total domination. The Soviet Union was providing supplies and manpower to keep Germany strong. The United States had refused to join the fight. When the Germans lost the Battle of Britain, Hitler made a fatal decision. On June 22, 1941, he launched Operation Barbarossa to attack the Soviet Union. Hitler was convinced he could conquer his ally. He was wrong.

- ➡ Hitler saw the communist Soviet Union as a natural enemy, even when he signed a treaty with its leader, Stalin.

- ➡ Hitler saw the land controlled by Stalin as a place where the Aryan race could expand and grow for generations.

- ➡ Hitler knew the Soviet army was poorly trained. He believed they would be easy to defeat.

Betrayal of Stalin

◆ Germany invaded the Soviet Union in 1941 from three directions: Leningrad in the north, Moscow in the center, and Stalingrad in the south.

STAT FACT In a single week, Germany captured **200 SQUARE MILES** of Soviet territory, destroyed **4,000** aircraft, and killed, wounded, or captured **600,000** Soviet Red Army troops.

◆ By the end of six-month-long Operation Barbarossa, more than 800,000 Russians had been killed. Another 6 million had been wounded or captured. But Germany lost 775,000 men and found themselves surrounded by survivors hungry for revenge. Stalin soon joined the Allies to seal Hitler's fate.

Preparing for D-Day

→ The Allies knew that to win World War II, they would have to take France back from Hitler. In late 1943, they planned Operation Overlord, also known as D-Day. It would take place in the Normandy region on June 6, 1944.

PERSON TO KNOW **GENERAL DWIGHT D. EISENHOWER** was appointed Supreme Allied Commander of the Allied Expeditionary Force for the D-Day invasion.

→ British Prime Minister Winston Churchill wanted to join Eisenhower at Normandy. But the general finally convinced him to remain in London.

Eisenhower with troops

★ D-Day isn't actually the name of the mission. "D-Day" is a placeholder, a temporary name for all missions before they begin. It helps keep secret missions secure. "H-Hour" is used for the time a mission is set to begin.

STAT FACT Why was planning so important? D-Day would involve **156,115** American, British, and Canadian troops; **6,939** ships and landing vessels; **2,395** airplanes; and **867** gliders. Success depended on very careful coordination.

Ships gathering for D-Day

➜ Churchill and Roosevelt spent years planning D-Day. The odds were against them, so they tried to anticipate every problem in advance.

Battle of Normandy

⭐ To deceive the Nazis, Allied forces leaked false information about D-Day. They said the invasion would take place at Pas-de-Calais, the French coastline closest to England.

⭐ The Ghost Army was an expert team of special effects artists. They built fake inflatable tanks and used sound effects to make it look like troops were gathering somewhere else, while the real troops were preparing to invade beaches at Normandy.

The Battle of Normandy was supposed to happen on June 5, 1944, but bad weather delayed the attack 24 hours.

➧ In the early morning of June 6, thousands of paratroopers dropped by air into Normandy to prepare for the soldiers coming by sea. They secured bridges and exit roads.

★ The Allied soldiers who landed in boats hit five stretches of beach. The beaches were code-named Utah, Omaha, Gold, Juno, and Sword.

Allied soldiers landing on the beach

After five days of fighting, the beaches and the harbors of Normandy were secured by the Allies. In the weeks that followed, they continued further into France with more troops, vehicles, and equipment to liberate the country from Nazi occupation.

Battle of the Bulge

→ Hitler knew he was in trouble when the Allies took France back from the Nazis. He launched one last major assault on December 16, 1944, in the Ardennes Forest of Belgium.

STAT FACT The Battle of the Bulge was fought over six weeks during frigid winter temperatures. German troops fought exhausted American troops across **85 MILES** of rugged wilderness, as fog prevented help from the US Air Force.

Hitler had hoped to force the Allies back to Great Britain so he could negotiate a new treaty giving the Nazis immeasurable power.

→ Hitler believed his attack would surprise and confuse the Allies. He thought it would take General Eisenhower weeks to plan his response to the assault. The American army was caught off guard, but Eisenhower had full authority to respond.

STAT FACT One in eight American soldiers defended the Ardennes Forest in the biggest battle the US Army has ever fought. More than **600,000** American troops were present. They were victorious by January 25, 1945.

★ Famed author Kurt Vonnegut fought in the Battle of the Bulge and was taken prisoner by the Germans. His 1969 novel *Slaughterhouse-Five* was inspired by the experience.

Kurt Vonnegut's
army photo

German Cities in Ruin

◆ In February 1945, US president Roosevelt and British prime minister Churchill promised Soviet premier Joseph Stalin they would continue to bomb German cities to pave the way for Soviet soldiers advancing in Germany.

Dresden before bombing

The British Royal Air Force dropped 4,000 tons of explosives on the German city of Dresden from February 13 to February 15, 1945.

STAT FACT More than **25,000** people died in the Dresden firestorm. Those who weren't killed on impact suffocated after the explosions sucked oxygen from the air. The German cities of Cologne, Hamburg, and Berlin soon suffered the same fate.

The Allies thought attacking military targets alone would not be enough to break the Nazi hold on Germany. They bombed all German industry, hoping to teach the German people a lesson and force surrender.

Almost as soon Prime Minister Churchill ordered the air strikes, he began to doubt his decision. He wrote that "the question of bombing of German cities simply for the sake of increasing terror ... should be reviewed."

Before the bombing, Dresden was called "the jewel box" of Germany because it was so beautiful. All that beauty was turned to rubble.

Dresden after bombing

Hitler's Last Days

◗ As world domination slipped from Hitler's reach in January 1945, he hid in a bombproof underground shelter in Berlin. The Allies were nearing Germany from the west, as Russian soldiers approached from the east.

◗ Hitler dictated his will to his personal secretary in the late hours of April 28 and into the early morning hours of April 29.

◗ Hitler married his girlfriend, Eva Braun, in the bunker. Propaganda minister Joseph Goebbels and his wife were the witnesses to the union. As they celebrated the wedding, Hitler spoke of happier times in his past.

Hitler and Eva Braun

◆ When Hitler heard the Italian dictator Mussolini and his girlfriend, Claretta Petacci, had been executed by their Italian enemies, he swore he'd never be taken. He ordered his bodyguards to destroy his personal papers and kill his dog, Blondi.

◆ After their final goodbyes, Adolf Hitler and his new bride retired to their private room in the bunker. Eva swallowed a poison pill and Hitler took his own life using a Walther PPK pistol.

Hitler's bunker

The dead bodies of Hitler and Braun were doused in gasoline and burned in the garden outside the bunker.

Atomic Bomb Debate

◆ In July 1945, President Harry S. Truman learned the United States had developed a new weapon. The atomic bomb was ready to use, and it would cause death on a massive scale.

◆ Truman felt he had four choices to end the war with Japan. He could authorize traditional bombings of Japanese cities. He could invade Japan. He could drop the bomb on an unpopulated island. Or, finally, he could drop the atomic bomb on Japan.

Traditional bombing caused destruction in Tokyo

STAT FACT Traditional bombing between 1944 and 1945 had killed **333,000** Japanese citizens in Tokyo and Okinawa. It wounded **473,000** more. But Japan refused to surrender.

◆ Dropping an atomic bomb on an unpopulated Pacific island would cause fewer casualties, but Truman feared Japan would still refuse to surrender. A ground invasion would kill thousands of Americans soldiers and citizens, so he ruled that out, too.

◆ On August 6, 1945, Truman gave the controversial order. The *Enola Gay*, a US B-29 bomber plane, dropped America's first atomic bomb on Hiroshima. A second atomic bomb was dropped on Nagasaki on August 9.

Enola Gay

STAT FACT In the atomic blasts, temperatures soared to **5,400** degrees Fahrenheit. Birds burst into flames in midair. Asphalt boiled. As many as **226,000** people died in both cities, most of them civilians.

Soviet War on Japan

→ The Soviet Union declared war on Japan in 1945. On August 8, one million Soviet soldiers poured into Japanese-occupied Manchuria, China.

Soviet soldiers in Manchuria

STAT FACT The Japanese Army commanded more than **1 MILLION** troops, **6,260** guns and mortar shells, **1,155** tanks, **1,900** aircraft, and **25** ships in and near Manchuria.

→ Japan was well armed but caught off guard by the Soviet invasion. They thought the Soviets were busy with the German fight in Europe. They didn't expect to face them in battle until the spring of 1946.

The Mongolian People's Revolutionary Army fought alongside the Russians during the invasion. They hoped to end Japan's occupation of China and North Korea.

Emperor Hirohito begged his military to surrender after so many Japanese soldiers were killed by the Soviets. They did not agree to his request until after the United States bombed Nagasaki.

Japan surrendered on August 15, 1945. The formal signing ceremony was held on September 2, 1945 on the USS *Missouri* in Tokyo Bay, Japan. General Douglas McArthur accepted the surrender and the Allied Occupation of Japan began.

Japanese Minister of Foreign Affairs signs the surrender papers

America Reacts

On August 14, 1945, President Truman announced that Japan had surrendered. The war had finally ended.

People celebrating Japan's surrender in New York

US ships were headed to Japan when President Truman announced the war was over. They were ordered to turn around and head home. Soldiers cried with relief.

★ Some young children had never seen their fathers, who had been fighting overseas. They would soon meet the brave men who had fought for their freedom.

Rationing of food and gasoline would finally end. A new normal was about to unfold. People prayed the peace would last.

All of America celebrated the end of World War II, but none with more energy than New York City.

⭐ **The Garment District was an area of New York City where clothes were made. Workers in this neighborhood made confetti out of tiny bits of cloth. They tossed it from windows. Other revelers tossed paper confetti.**

Confetti in the streets of New York City

STAT FACT **TWO MILLION** people filled **10** blocks near Times Square to share in the national joy and relief together.

➤ Across the United States, people flocked to church after the announcement of Japan's surrender. Special services were arranged in cities like Chicago.

CHAPTER 11

AFTERMATH OF WWII

After the war, citizens of the world were in a state of confusion. Huge portions of Europe and Asia had been bombed into rubble. Borders that had shifted after World War I had to shift once again. Allied forces replaced the Germans as occupying armies. And no one was sure how to restructure the world to make it safe. Avoiding a third world war was the challenge humanity now faced. How do you create a new world dedicated to freedom and peace after a war so bloody and fierce? The future of the world depended on finding the answers to that and other crucial questions.

➡ **Two billion people lived in the world in 1930. After World War II, 4 percent of the population was gone.**

➡ **The Allies took control of Germany and Japan in an effort to stop them from making war in the future.**

➡ **Tension between the Western Allies and the Soviets caused the Cold War, which lasted from 1947 to 1991.**

Death Toll

- The Axis and Allied powers caused between 70 and 85 million deaths worldwide.

World War II Memorial, Washington, DC

More civilians than soldiers died in World War II— almost twice as many.

STAT FACT The Soviet Union lost **24 MILLION** people. China lost nearly **20 MILLION** people. Germany lost almost **9 MILLION** people. Poland lost more than **5 MILLION** people. Japan lost more than **3 MILLION** people. The United States lost about **418,000** people. Great Britain and Italy each lost more than **450,000** people. France lost more than **500,000** people.

More than **6 MILLION** of the dead were European Jews killed in the Holocaust.

Rebuilding and Justice

◆ US general George
Marshall came up with
the European Recovery
Program, also known as
the Marshall Plan. He
proposed the United
States would provide
more than $15 billion to
help rebuild Europe after the war.

**Food distribution in Greece
under the Marshall Plan**

◆ After the war, Great Britain and France held their traditional
borders. The size of Germany was reduced significantly. The
Soviet Union controlled the Baltic States.

◆ Many Jews escaped to Palestine, a land in the Middle East
they considered their ancestral homeland. In 1947, there was
a plan to share Palestine by forming a Jewish state and an
Arab state. The plan was rejected, but Israel was proclaimed
an independent state in 1948. The battle for Palestinian
territory has continued ever since.

In August 1945, the International Military Tribunal was established in Nuremberg, Germany. The courts were charged with prosecuting military criminals for war crimes.

STAT FACT One of the most famous Nuremberg trials tried **22** German war criminals beginning on November 20, 1945. Almost a year later, **19** were found guilty. **TWELVE** were sentenced to death, **THREE** got life in prison, and **FOUR** were sentenced to 10 to 20 years in jail.

➡ The International Military Tribunal for the Far East was established in Tokyo in 1946. That court system tried Japanese officials accused of war crimes.

International Military Tribunal

The Atlantic Charter

TERM TO KNOW In August 1941, President Roosevelt and Prime Minister Churchill held a secret meeting to establish the **ATLANTIC CHARTER**. It was meant to identify and assist all nations opposed to the Axis powers.

★ The meeting to establish the Atlantic Charter was held in Newfoundland, Canada, by the Atlantic waters of Placentia Bay. The charter was designed to inspire lasting peace in the world.

Atlantic Charter Monument

➧ After the war ended in 1945, the Atlantic Charter expanded to become the United Nations. World leaders hoped it would establish peace and global stability. It had 51 member states when it was created.

STAT FACT Today, the United Nations has **193** member nations. Headquartered in New York City, it tries to prevent conflict, protect the peace, and provide humanitarian assistance for nations in need as a result of natural disasters or war.

United Nations members try to act as peacekeepers. They are sometimes successful, sometimes not.

The United Nations sought to guarantee peace when it was founded. Part of its mission now includes fighting global warming, disease, and other worldwide problems.

United Nations building in New York, New York

RESOURCES

Books

Bomb: The Race to Build—and Steal—the World's Most Dangerous Weapon by Steve Sheinkin, Squarefish, 2018.

Eyewitness World War II by Simon Adams, DK Publishing, 2014.

Spies, Code Breakers, and Secret Agents by Carole P. Roman, Rockridge Press, 2020.

World War II for Kids by Richard Panchyk, Chicago Review Press, 2001.

Websites

BBC World War II
BBC.CO.UK/history/worldwars/wwtwo

The Price of Freedom: Americans at War, Smithsonian Institute
AmHistory.SI.edu/militaryhistory

Spartacus Educational Encyclopedia of WW2
Spartacus-Educational.com/2WW.htm

Student Resources: National World War II Museum
NationalWW2Museum.org/students-teachers/student-resources

Museums

International Museum of World War II
8 Mercer Road, Natick, MA 01760
MuseumOfWorldWarII.org

National World War II Memorial
1750 Independence Ave. SW, Washington, DC 20024
WWIIMemorial.com

The National World War II Museum
945 Magazine Street, New Orleans, LA 70130
NationalWW2Museum.org

United States Holocaust Memorial Museum
100 Raoul Wallenberg Place SW, Washington, DC 20024
USHMM.org

Historical Sites

Anne Frank House: Amsterdam, Netherlands
AnneFrank.org/en

Auschwitz-Birkenau Memorial and Museum: Oswiecim, Poland
Auschwitz.org/en/

Hiroshima Peace Memorial and Museum: Hiroshima, Japan
HPMMuseum.jp/?lang=eng

Memorial to the Murdered Jews of Europe: Berlin, Germany
VisitBerlin.de/en/memorial-murdered-jews-europe

SELECTED REFERENCES

AeroTime Extra. 2016. "Spitfire: The Only Fighter Built Throughout WWII." *AeroTime Hub*, June 16. Aerotime.aero/23093-spitfire-the-only-fighter-built-wwii.

Army.mil Features. n.d. "Asian Americans & Pacific Islanders in the United States Army." Army.mil/asianpacificamericans/history/.

Axelrod, Josh. 2019. "A Century Later: The Treaty of Versailles and Its Rejection of Racial Equality." NPR *Code Switch*, August 11. NPR.org/sections/codeswitch/2019/08/11/742293305/a-century-later-the-treaty-of-versailles-and-its-rejection-of-racial-equality.

Bamford, Tyler. 2020. "Medal of Honor Recipient Daniel Inouye Led a Life of Service to His Country." New Orleans: The National WWII Museum, July 19. NationalWW2Museum.org/war/articles/medal-of-honor-recipient-daniel-inouye.

———. 2020. "The Most Fearsome Sight: The Atomic Bombing of Hiroshima." New Orleans: The National WWII Museum, August 6. NationalWW2Museum.org/war/articles/atomic-bomb-hiroshima.

Barber, Nicholas. 2021. "The Great Dictator: The Film That Dared to Laugh at Hitler." *BBC Culture*, February 5. BBC.com/culture/article/20210204-the-great-dictator-the-film-that-dared-to-laugh-at-hitler.

BBC Editors. 2020. "France Honours Six-Year-Old WW2 Resistance Agent." *BBC News*, November 12. BBC.com/news/world-europe-54919375.

———. 2014. "History - Noor Inayat Khan." BBC.co.uk/history/historic_figures/inayat_khan_noor.shtml.

Bernstein, Adam. 2011. "Nancy Wake, 'White Mouse' of World War II, Dies at 98." *The Washington Post*, August 9. WashingtonPost.com/local/obituaries/nancy-wake-white-mouse-of-world-war-ii-dies-at-98/2011/08/08/gIQABvPT5I_story.html.

Boissoneault, Lorraine. 2018. "The Nazi Werewolves Who Terrorized
   Allied Soldiers at the End of WWII." *Smithsonian Magazine*, October 30.
   SmithsonianMag.com/history/nazi-werewolves-who-terrorized-allied
   -soldiers-end-wwii-180970522.

Brockell, Gillian. 2020. "The Polish Hero Who Volunteered to Go to Auschwitz—
   and Warned the World about the Nazi Death Machine."
   The Washington Post, January 26. WashingtonPost.com/history/2020/01
   /26/pilecki-auschwitz-polish-resistance.

Butler, Stephanie. 2014. "How Hershey's Chocolate Helped Power Allied Troops
   During WWII." History.com, A&E Television Networks, Last updated August 7,
   2019. History.com/news/hersheys-chocolate-allied-d-day-rations-wwii.

Chan, Melissa. 2016. "'A Date Which Will Live in Infamy.' Read President
   Roosevelt's Pearl Harbor Address." *Time*, Last updated December 6, 2018.
   Time.com/4593483/pearl-harbor-franklin-roosevelt-infamy-speech-attack.

Chivers, C. J. 2014. "A Veteran's Chemical Burns Expanded Military Doctors'
   Knowledge, but His Care Faltered." *The New York Times*, December 30.
   NYTimes.com/2014/12/31/us/veterans-chemical-burns-expanded-military
   -doctors-knowledge-but-his-care-faltered.html.

Clark, Alexis. 2020. "Black Americans Who Served in WWII Faced Segregation
   Abroad and at Home." History.com, A&E Television Networks, August 5.
   History.com/news/black-soldiers-world-war-ii-discrimination.

Cooper, Pen. 2015. "37 Military Uniforms Worn by Soldiers During
   World War II." *History Daily*, September 23. Historydaily.org/world-war-2
   -military-uniforms.

The Daily Journal. 2002. "135,000 People Died in Firebomb Attack on Dresden."
   Last updated October 14, 2013. Daily-Journal.com/news/local/135-000-
   people-died-in-firebomb-attack-on-dresden/article_7f22d6f8-5f44-509d
   -8967-dc086c1799e6.html.

Daley, Jason. 2017. "WWII Enigma Machine Found at Flea Market Sells for
   $51,000." *Smithsonian Magazine*, July 13. SmithsonianMag.com/smart-news
   /wwii-enigma-machine-found-flea-market-sells-51000-180964053.

Door, Robert F. 2010. "Actor Clark Gable Served in Uniform, Flew Combat Missions in World War II." *Defense Media Network*, August 11. DefenseMediaNetwork.com/stories/clark-gable-served-in-uniform -flew-combat-missions-in-world-war-ii.

Gross, Terry. 2016. "Creamed, Canned and Frozen: How the Great Depression Revamped U.S. Diets." NPR's *Fresh Air*, August 15. NPR.org/sections /thesalt/2016/08/15/489991111/creamed-canned-and-frozen-how-the -great-depression-changed-u-s-diets.

The Guardian Editors. 1945. "From the Archive: Hitler's Deadly Secret Weapons Come to Light." *The Guardian*, June 28. TheGuardian.com/news /1945/jun/29/mainsection.fromthearchive.

———. 2014. "Jerry Roberts Obituary." *The Guardian*, Last updated April 1, 2014. TheGuardian.com/world/2014/mar/31/jerry-roberts.

Guise, Kim. 2020. "Medal of Honor Recipient Vernon Baker: 'Set the Example.'" New Orleans: The National World War II Museum, September 25. NationalWW2Museum.org/war/articles/medal-of-honor-recipient -vernon-baker.

Hambling, David. 2020. "The Most Important Battles of World War II." *Popular Mechanics*, October 14. PopularMechanics.com/military/g2652/most-important -battles-world-war-ii.

Harry S. Truman National Historic Site, Manhattan Project National Historical Park. 2017. "Harry S. Truman's Decision to Use the Atomic Bomb." *National Park Service*, U.S. Department of the Interior, Last updated October 25, 2017. NPS.gov/articles/trumanatomicbomb.htm.

History.com Editors. 2009. "Adolf Hitler Commits Suicide." History.com, A&E Television Networks, Last updated April 28, 2020. History.com/this-day-in -history/adolf-hitler-commits-suicide.

———. 2009. "Beer Hall Putsch." History.com, A&E Television Networks, Last updated August 21, 2018. History.com/topics/germany/beer-hall-putsch.

———. 2009. "Britain and France Declare War on Germany." History.com, A&E Television Networks, Last updated September 1, 2020. History.com /this-day-in-history/britain-and-france-declare-war-on-germany.

————. 2009. "Erwin Rommel." History.com, A&E Television Networks, Last updated August 21, 2018. History.com/topics/world-war-ii/erwin-rommel-erwin.

————. 2010. "Japan Surrenders; World War II Ends." History.com, A&E Television Networks, Last updated May 14, 2021. History.com/this-day-in-history/japan-surrenders.

————. 2009. "Japanese Internment Camps." History.com, A&E Television Networks, Last updated April 27, 2021. History.com/topics/world-war-ii/japanese-american-relocation.

————. 2009. "Marshall Plan." History.com, A&E Television Networks, Last updated June 5, 2020. History.com/topics/world-war-ii/marshall-plan-1.

————. 2009. "Soviet Master Spy is Hanged by the Japanese." History.com, A&E Television Networks, Last updated November 5, 2020. History.com/this-day-in-history/soviet-master-spy-is-hanged-by-the-japanese.

————. 2010. "Soviets Declare War on Japan; Invade Manchuria." History.com, A&E Television Networks, Last updated August 5, 2020. History.com/this-day-in-history/soviets-declare-war-on-japan-invade-manchuria.

————. 2018. "United Nations." History.com, A&E Television Networks, Last updated August 21, 2018. History.com/topics/world-war-ii/united-nations.

Imperial War Museums. n.d. "Second World War Weapons That Failed." IWM.org.uk/history/second-world-war-weapons-that-failed.

King, Gilbert. 2011. "Behind Enemy Lines with Violette Szabo." *Smithsonian Magazine*, December 6. SmithsonianMag.com/history/behind-enemy-lines-with-violette-szabo-1896571.

Lauder, Val. 2020. "D-Day and General Eisenhower's Greatest Decision." *The Saturday Evening Post*, June 3. SaturdayEveningPost.com/2020/06/d-day-and-general-eisenhowers-greatest-decision.

Lavin, Frank. 2019. "The Battle of the Bulge Was Hitler's Last Gamble." *The Wall Street Journal*, Dow Jones & Company, December 7. WSJ.com/articles/the-battle-of-the-bulge-was-hitlers-last-gamble-11575694860.

Lengel, Ed. 2020. "Forgotten Fights: Malta's Faith, Hope, and Charity, 1940." New Orleans: The National World War II Museum, August 24. NationalWW2Museum.org/war/articles/british-biplanes-faith-hope -charity-1940.

Little, Becky. 2018. "This Teenager Killed Nazis with Her Sister During WWII." History.com, A&E Television Networks, Last updated February 22, 2021. History.com/news/dutch-resistance-teenager-killed-nazis-freddie -oversteegen.

Lockie, Alex. 2017. "Hitler's Secret Nazi War Machines of World War II." *Business Insider*, May 27. BusinessInsider.com/nazi-war-machines-of-world -war-ii-2017-5#a-rocket-powered-plane-that-was-nearly-300-mph-quicker -than-the-fastest-aircraft-around-6.

Loftus, Geoff. 2016. "America's Response to Pearl Harbor Serves as a Leadership Lesson for All." *Forbes Magazine*, December 7. Forbes.com/sites /geoffloftus/2016/12/07/pearl-harbor-leadership-lessons/?sh=1b830b625f27.

Martin, Kali. 2020. "Louisiana Spotlight: Corporal Albert Porche, 99th Fighter Squadron." New Orleans: The National World War II Museum, June 16. NationalWW2Museum.org/war/articles/louisianacorporal-albert-porche -99th-fighter-squadron.

Marton, Kati. 2019. "Remembering a Woman Who Was a Leader of the French Resistance." *The New York Times*, March 12. NYTimes.com/2019/03/12/books /review/lynne-olson-madame-fourcades-secret-war.html.

The National WWII Museum. n.d. "Research Starters: Worldwide Deaths in World War II." NationalWW2Museum.org/students-teachers/student-resources /research-starters/research-starters-worldwide-deaths-world-war.

Pacific Battleship Center. n.d. "Learn about Our Mascot, Vicky the Dog." Los Angeles: Battleship USS *Iowa* Museum. PacificBattleship.com/learn-the -history/the-story-of-victory-the-dog.

PBS.org Editors. n.d. "Book Burnings in Germany, 1933." PBS.org/wgbh /americanexperience/features/goebbels-burnings.

————. n.d. "Groups During the American Civil Rights Movement." PBS.org /wgbh/americanexperience/features/eyesontheprize-groups-during-american -civil-rights-movement.

Roberts, Jerry. n.d. "How Lorenz Was Different from Enigma." TheHistoryPress. co.uk/articles/how-lorenz-was-different-from-enigma.

Roos, Dave. 2019. "D-Day: Facts on the Epic 1944 Invasion That Changed the Course of WWII." History.com, A&E Television Networks, Last updated June 4, 2020. History.com/news/d-day-normandy-wwii-facts#.

Rossen, Jake. 2016. "The Jewish Psychic Who Tricked Hitler." *Mental Floss*, April 25. MentalFloss.com/article/78979/jewish-psychic-who-tricked-hitler.

Shirley, Craig, and Scott Mauer. 2019. "The Attack on Pearl Harbor United Americans Like No Other Event in Our History." *The Washington Post*, March 1. WashingtonPost.com/posteverything/wp/2016/12/07/the-attack-on-pearl -harbor-united-americans-like-no-other-event-in-our-history.

Siddiqui, Usaid. 2020. "Noor Inayat Khan: The Forgotten Muslim Princess Who Fought Nazis." *Al Jazeera*, October 28. AlJazeera.com/features/2020 /10/28/noor-inayat-khan.

Siegphyl. 2015. "Crafty Gadgets and Famous Spies of WWII." *War History Online*, February 5. WarHistoryOnline.com/war-articles/crafty-gadgets-tricks -famous-wwii-spies.html.

Snyder, Timothy. 2019. "How Hitler Pioneered 'Fake News.'" *The New York Times*, October 16. NYTimes.com/2019/10/16/opinion/hitler-speech-1919.html.

Sutton, Matthew Avery. 2019. "The U.S. Recruited Missionaries as Spies During World War II. Their Stories are Only Now Being Told." *Time*, September 24. Time.com/5684518/missionaries-spies.

Szoldra, Paul. 2017. "The First 'Battle' of World War II Was a Nazi War Crime." *Business Insider*, September 1. BusinessInsider.com/the-first-battle-of-world -war-ii-was-a-nazi-war-crime-2015-9.

Taylor, Alan. 2011. "World War II: After the War." *The Atlantic*, Atlantic Media Company, October 30. TheAtlantic.com/photo/2011/10/world-war-ii-after -the-war/100180.

Team Mighty. 2015. "21 Rare and Weird Facts about World War II." *Business Insider*, August 8. BusinessInsider.com/21-rare-and-weird-facts-about-world-war-2-2015-8#5-polish-catholic-midwife-stanisawa-leszczyska-delivered-3000-babies-at-the-auschwitz-concentration-camp-during-the-holocaust-in-occupied-poland-5.

Tucker, Reed. 2019. "Hollywood Legend Audrey Hepburn Was a WWII Resistance Spy." *New York Post*, April 9. NYPost.com/2019/04/09/hollywood-legend-audrey-hepburn-was-a-wwii-resistance-spy.

Twomey, Steve. 2016. "How (Almost) Everyone Failed to Prepare for Pearl Harbor." *Smithsonian Magazine* (December). SmithsonianMag.com/history/how-almost-everyone-failed-prepare-pearl-harbor-1-180961144.

United States Holocaust Memorial Museum. n.d. "Holocaust Encyclopedia: Paul Von Hindenburg." Encyclopedia.USHMM.org/content/en/article/paul-von-hindenburg.

———. 2020. "Holocaust Encyclopedia: Postwar Trials." Last updated October 26, 2020. Encyclopedia.USHMM.org/content/en/article/war-crimes-trials.

University of California. 2009. "Everyday Life During World War II." Calisphere.org/exhibitions/41/everyday-life-during-world-war-ii.

Waxman, Olivia B. 2017. "The Bear Who Became a Cigarette-Smoking, Beer-Drinking World War II Hero." *Time*, April 8. Time.com/4731787/wojtek-the-bear-history.

———. 2019. "What to Know about the Origins of Fascism's Brutal Ideology." *Time*, March 22. Time.com/5556242/what-is-fascism.

Wolf, Walter III. 2020. "Secret Agents, Secret Armies: The Short Happy Life of the OSS." New Orleans: The National WWII Museum, May 14. NationalWW2Museum.org/war/articles/wwii-secret-agents-the-oss.

ABOUT THE AUTHOR

 **KELLY MILNER HALLS** has written five books about World War II for young readers. She believes if we learn the lessons of the worst war in history, we may be able to prevent it from happening again. She also loves other nonfiction topics, including the *Titanic*, Bigfoot, UFOs, ghosts, and just about anything to do with animals, especially horses, dogs, cats, sea slugs, and tardigrades. Find out more about Kelly at her website: WondersOfWeird.com

ABOUT THE ILLUSTRATOR

 **KATY DOCKRILL**, an honors graduate of the Ontario College of Art and Design, is an award-winning illustrator with a passion for line. She brings the simplest drawings to life with her fresh, cheerful, and playfully detailed brushwork, a style her international and local clients expect and love. She shares a creative home in Toronto with her husband, daughter, and a cat named Kitty.